Study Guide to Accompa

World Religions

❖ Second Edition

Warren Matthews
Old Dominion University

Prepared by
David C. Prejsnar
Community College of Philadelphia

West Publishing Company
Minneapolis/St. Paul New York Los Angeles San Francisco

WEST'S COMMITMENT TO THE ENVIRONMENT

In 1906, West Publishing Company began recycling materials left over from the production of books. This began a tradition of efficient and responsible use of resources. Today, up to 95% of our legal books and 70% of our college texts and school texts are printed on recycled, acid-free stock. West also recycles nearly 22 million pounds of scrap paper annually—the equivalent of 181,717 trees. Since the 1960s, West has devised ways to capture and recycle waste inks, solvents, oils, and vapors created in the printing process. We also recycle plastics of all kinds, wood, glass, corrugated cardboard, and batteries, and have eliminated the use of Styrofoam book packaging. We at West are proud of the longevity and the scope of our commitment to the environment.

Production, Prepress, Printing and Binding by West Publishing Company.

TEXT IS PRINTED ON 10% POST
CONSUMER RECYCLED PAPER

PRINTED WITH
SOY INK

Printed in the United States of America
02 01 00 99 98 97 96 95 8 7 6 5 4 3 2 1 0

ISBN 0–314–05426–X

Contents

To the Student

Your study of world religion is an enterprise that I hope will at once excite and bewilder, provoke and calm, challenge and enlighten you. To study the religious experiences of human beings is to see both the cruelty of which people are capable and yet to gain hope for the future. Your course in world religions will teach you about human history, how different peoples have searched for an Absolute, how they have tried to explain why bad things happen to them and how they have expressed these insights in their words, in their art and in their actions.

Your textbook, World Religions, 2nd Edition by Warren Matthews, is designed to be a readable and exciting introduction to the field of religious studies. It is written to allow easy comparisons of the beliefs and practices of the different religious traditions. This second edition of the study guide has been revised to build on the critical thinking and writing approach found in the first edition. It is designed to help you learn and apply the material you will read in the textbook. I hope it will be of assistance to you in a number of ways. The first three parts of each chapter in the guide are designed to give you an overview of each chapter in the textbook, and present you with standards to help measure how well you are mastering the material in the textbook. Part four challenges you to apply some of the information you have gained in the textbook to the analysis of primary source religious documents. The type of analysis you do here should also assist you in preparing for examinations and paper assignments. Parts five and six, along with the section on analyzing texts, should provide you with the tools for evaluating your understanding of the material in the run-up to examinations. You will be able to design your own practice examination. Finally, and, in my own view most importantly, parts seven, eight and nine of this guide are designed to take you beyond the examination. These sections will help you to work on your critical thinking skills: how to use skills such as analysis, synthesis and comparison to explore the truly exciting problems in the field of religious studies. They will also raise provocative problems for which there are no easy answers. In addition, these sections will challenge you to explore religious experience outside the classroom. Open-ended, critical and committed exploration is the type of learning that will endure long after dates and names have faded from memory.

You have probably already discovered methods of studying that help you organize material and develop your thoughts. If this is the case, follow the suggestions on how to use this guide that compliment what you already do well. The points that follow are only meant as suggestions. If, on the other hand, you have a difficult time preparing for and doing well on exams and essay papers, then you might want to try sticking to the step by step process outlined below. After you have mastered the skills required in the various steps, you can begin to alter them to fit your individual strengths and weaknesses.

Another point to take into consideration when deciding how to use this study guide is how your instructor has structured his or her course. The type of material your instructor emphasizes and the type of examination he or she will be giving may mean that you will find some parts of this guide more beneficial than others. This book contains a range of practice questions, so use those questions that will best prepare you for your exams.

One final suggestion is to write essays, to write research papers, but by all means to write. Regardless of the type of examination your instructor will be giving, spend time working on Parts Six through Nine of each chapter. These sections ask you to write essay questions and to examine the implications of what you have studied in the textbook and in class. More than an end in itself, writing helps you synthesize and analyze information. When you force yourself to write down your ideas, you will be able to better evaluate how much you understand. In addition, writing on these topics will reinforce your memory and aid in the retention of information.

Here are some suggestions on how to use this study guide:

1. Review the Learning Objectives to see which ones you already know. Check off in the book those you think you can accomplish. Keep in mind those you have not mastered.

2. Skim through the vocabulary list. I would suggest comparing the list to the textbook glossary. Check off on the study guide list those items that are in the glossary; these are probably the most important terms. The vocabulary list in this book is meant to be more exhaustive. The order of the terms in the list should roughly parallel the order in which they occur in the textbook.

3. Read the chapter in the textbook. I would suggest that you develop a system for highlighting or making notes that works for you. I think that writing notes in the margins is better than highlighting, since it gives you an opportunity to jot down your ideas and reactions. Using stars or some other symbols will allow you to grade the importance of each passage. Write down any points you did not understand, and look them up later. Write down any thoughts or comments on the reading; these may be ideas upon which you can build when write your paper.

4. Reread in the book, very quickly, the items you designated as most important.

5. Return to the study guide. Go through the Guided Review, writing down the answer in each blank. The Guided Review parallels the book, so you can easily check your answers.

6. Pick at least one of the texts in the Analyzing Texts section. Try to apply the material in the textbook, especially the selections from primary texts, to these primary documents. If you have time, write out your analysis. At the end of each chapter in this guide you will find the references for these texts. If you want to do further research on any of these topics, most of these books should be available in a good college library.

7. Give yourself a practice test in order to evaluate your understanding. One of the best ways to prepare for exams is to simulate, as much as possible, the actual examination conditions. Find out what type of questions the instructor usually includes on the exam. Construct a practice examination, using the Self-Test section, one or more essay questions and one of the texts. Try to replicate the examination conditions in time allowed, and access to materials. When you finish the practice exam, check the Answer Key at the end of the chapter. Look up the definitions in the textbook. Critique your essay, looking at how you can improve your writing style and substance.

8. Read through the "Confronting Issues and Answers" section. This section in each chapter examines an issue that has contemporary significance for that particular religious tradition. Consider each issue and how members of that tradition might respond to the issue. You could use this section for brainstorming different ideas, or you could use the issue as the topic for a discussion or a research paper.

9. Read the "Essay for a Deeper Consideration" section. This section is designed to help you improve your writing and analytical skills. Read the "Tips" for each question and try to incorporate them into your essay writing.

10. Finally, you might want to try out one or more of the "Projects for Developing Religious Empathy". These projects are designed to be done easily and in a college environment. They are not designed to convert, but rather to expand your awareness of the range of religious traditions.

Good luck! You will have to work hard to succeed in this course, but you can do it. I hope this study guide allows you to accomplish this task and to make each faith come alive.

Acknowledgments

This study guide reflects my experiences teaching undergraduates about the religions of India, Japan, China, the Near East and the West. I would like to thank all my colleagues who have over the years given me suggestions on teaching and insights into research. Many of their approaches and suggestions have percolated into this guide, in one form or another. I would especially like to thank my colleagues in the NEH Cultural Traditions Projects at Community College of Philadelphia where some of the ideas underlying this guide were debated. A very special note of thanks has to go to Edward Forman, my Co-Project Director and once and future teaching partner. I hope some of his insights into teaching and the Humanities has seeped into this volume. Johanna Land and Linda Poirier at West Publishing deserve my special thanks for their understanding and patience.

Finally, I would like to dedicate this Second Edition of the Study Guide to the memory of my wife, Caroline, whose benevolence taught me so much, and to my daughter, Katie.

Introduction

PART ONE LEARNING OBJECTIVES

Doing these exercises, in conjunction with reading the textbook, should help you to achieve many of the following objectives. Read them and see how many you already have mastered; then study the following terms and concepts, and work through the exercises. After you have completed all the exercises, review the objectives again.

You should be able to:

1. Explain some of the reasons for the interest in the study of world religions among university and college students.

2. Name, define and group some of the important features and concepts used in religious studies, and give examples from different religious traditions of each of these features.

3. Understand the organization of each chapter of the textbook, and the purpose of the different sections of each chapter.

4. Discuss the problem of tension between neutral objectivity and religious involvement as it relates to the academic study of world religions in a secular setting.

5. Cite and analyze a number of definitions of "religion"

that have been advanced by prominent scholars of religion.

6. Cite and analyze four different types of definitions of "religion", and give an example of each type of definition.

7. Formulate your own definition of "religion", and give some initial examples of how your definition could be applied to religious beliefs and practices.

PART TWO TERMS AND INDIVIDUALS

a) Terms and Concepts

sacred
secular
sacred stories
epics
scriptures
rites of passage
religious drama
worldview
anthropology
cuneiform
Absolute
symbol
culture
essential definitions
descriptive definitions
profane
sacred space
myths
sacred writings
rituals
dance
history of religions
archaeology
sociology
hieroglyphics
history
religion
normative definitions
functional definitions

b) Individuals

Mircea Eliade
Walter Huston Clark
Ludwig Feuerbach
Thomas Luckmann
Clifford Geertz
Sigmund Freud
Wilfred Cantwell Smith
William James
Paul Tillich
Karl Marx
Peter Berger
Emile Durkheim
Rudolph Otto

PART THREE GUIDED REVIEW

1. There are many reasons why there is today strong interest in the study of world religions. What might be at least three reasons for interest in the study of world religions (use either ideas of your own or examples from the textbook):

a. ____.
b. ____.
c. ____.

2. Religious study uses the concepts of the sacred and the profane to help analyze and study religion. The "sacred" can be understood as ___________________, while the "profane" can be seen as ____________________.

3. Two examples mentioned in the textbook of a sacred space would be ________________ and ____________________.

4. Sacred stories that try to explain the beginnings of peoples or the world can be called _____________ stories. These would be an example of a type of story called a ______.

5. Long, narrative poems about the feats of legendary or historical heroes are known as ______________.

6. Sacred writings which are held to be authoritative to a particular religious tradition are termed ________________.

7. The very process of writing and reading have often been considered ___________ by many peoples and traditions.

8. A ritual can be defined as ___________________________.

9. Religious rituals are performed on many different occasions. Three examples of such occasions might be _________________, ___________________, and ______________.

10. An example of a sacred dance might be ________________ ____

11. The Christian celebrations of Easter and Pentecost can be seen as examples of _________________________.

12. That branch of religious studies that focuses on the origin and development of religious traditions over time is _______________________________.

13. Among the writing systems that scholars have had to decipher are the picture writing of Egypt called ____________________, and the wedge-shaped characters of Mesopotamia called ______________________.

14. The majority of religious traditions have a belief in ____________________, the highest reality upon which all else depends.

15. The author argues that most religions see a central problem which humans must address, and, in addition, posit a __________________ to this problem.

16. The concept of _________________ prompts one to refrain from making evaluative judgments about particular religions.

17. Scholars, in trying to understand the beliefs and views of adherents of different religious traditions, need _____________________, the sharing and appreciation of their emotions and faith.

18. Walter Huston Clark described "religion" as "the inner experience of the individual when he senses a _____________". The best evidence of religion is when the individual "attempts to harmonize his life with the ________________".

19. Paul Tillich argued that religion can be understood in terms of a person's ___________________, and this should not be a particular manifestation which he terms _______________.

20. Definitions of religion which attempt to prescribe what religion ought to be can be called _____________ definitions.

21. Essential definitions of religion attempt to ___________ _______________________________, while functional definitions attempt to ____.

22. The type of definition of "religion" found in a dictionary is likely to be a _________________ definition.

23. Rudolph Otto argued that religion is the feeling of _________________ in the presence of the Holy.

24. Sigmund Freud in one of his writings considers religion to be an _____________, by which he meant a belief growing out of a deep wish or need.

25. Wilfred Cantwell Smith argues that the concept of "religion" should be replaced with the more appropriate term ________________.

PART FOUR REVIEW OF THE STRUCTURE OF THE TEXTBOOK

Each chapter of the textbook is organized into a number of different sections. Each of these sections is designed to acquaint the student with a different aspect of the religious tradition. After reading the section of the Introduction that explains the organization of each chapter, write in your own words, a short description of the function and nature of each section.

1. Historical Development - ______________________________
____.

2. Worldview - ______________________________
____.

a. Absolute ______________________________
____.

b. The World ______________________________
____.

c. Humans ______________________________
____.

d. The Problem for Humans ______________________________
____.

e. The Solution for Humans ______________________________
____.

f. Community and Ethics ______________________________
____.

g. An Interpretation of History ______________________________
____.

h. Rituals and Symbols ______________________________
____.

i. Life After Death ______________________________
____.

j. Relationship to Other Religions ______________________________
____.

3. A Deeper Consideration ______________________________
____.

4. Resources for Study ______________________________
____.

PART FIVE ANALYZING TEXTS

Below are two texts that were not in the textbook. Both texts, however, do contain ideas and concepts with which you should be familiar after reading the textbook and studying the selections in the textbook from primary religious documents. Read each text carefully, compare it to the primary documents in the text and try to analyze each by answering the following questions: What are the main ideas in the text? What viewpoint or viewpoints might the author of the text represent? Is it possible to identify the specific thinker, discipline, movement, tradition or work from which the text derives? What intellectual, literary, social, cultural or historical influences are reflected in the text? For each of your conclusions, try to point to specific evidence in the text (e.g. terms, ideas, arguments, writing style, etc.) which supports your conclusion. Be careful that your conclusions do not exceed the evidence upon which they rest.

TEXT ONE

> Culture consists of the totality of man's products. Some of these are material, others are not. Man produces tools of every conceivable kind, by means of which he modifies his physical environment and bends nature to his will. Man also produces language, and on its foundation and by means of it, a towering edifice of symbols that permeate every aspect of his life. .... Society is constituted and maintained by acting human beings. It has no reality, apart from this activity. Its patterns, always relative in time and space, are not given in nature, nor can they be deduced in any specific manner from the "nature of man". What appears at any particular historical moment as "human nature" is itself a product of man's world-building activity. . . . The "stuff" out of which society and all its formations are made is human meanings externalized in human activity. . . . . It may now be understandable if the proposition is made that the socially constructed world is, above all, an ordering of experience. A meaningful order, or <u>nomos</u>, is imposed upon the discrete experiences and meanings of individuals. To say that society is a world-building enterprise is to say that it is ordering, or nomizing, activity. . . . . Religion is the human

> enterprise by which a sacred cosmos is established. Put differently, religion is cosmization in a sacred mode. By sacred is meant here a quality of mysterious and awesome power, other than man and yet related to him, which is believed to reside in certain objects of experience.. . . Every society is engaged in the never completed enterprise of building a humanly meaningful world. Cosmization implies the identification of this humanly meaningful world with the world as such, the former now being grounded in the latter, reflecting it or being derived from it in its fundamental structures. . . . . It can thus be said that religion has played a strategic part in the human enterprise of world-building. Religion implies the farthest reach of man's self-externalization, of his infusion of reality with his own meanings. Religion implies that human order is projected into the totality of being. Put differently, religion is the audacious attempt to conceive of the entire universe as being humanly significant. [1]

TEXT TWO

> Meanwhile the very fact that [proposed definitions of "religion"] are so many and so different from one another is enough to prove that the word "religion" cannot stand for any single principle or essence, but rather is a collective name. The theorizing mind tends always to the oversimplification of its materials. . . . Let us not fall immediately into a one-sided view of our subject, but let us rather admit freely at the outset that we may very likely find no one essence, but many characters which may alternately be equally important to religion. . . . At the outset we are struck by one great partition which divides the religious field. On the one side of it lies institutional, on the other personal religion. As M. P. Sabatier says, one branch of religion keeps the divinity, another keeps man most in view. . . . Now in these lectures I propose to ignore the institutional branch entirely, to say nothing of the ecclesiastical organization, to consider as little as possible the systematic theology and the ideas about the gods themselves, and to confine myself as far as I can to personal religion pure and simple. . . . . Religion, therefore, as I now ask you arbitrarily to take it, shall mean for us the feelings, acts, and experiences of individual men in their solitude, so far as they apprehend themselves to stand in relation to whatever they may consider the divine. [2]

PART SIX SELF-TEST

A) Definitions and Descriptions - Write your own definition or description of each of the following terms. After completing the self-test, check your answer with the definition or description given in the textbook.

1. History of Religions ______________________________.

2. Myth ______________________________.

3. Profane ______________________________.

4. Scripture ______________________________.

5. Normative definition of religion ______________________________.

6. Sacred ______________________________.

7. Functional definition of religion ______________________________.

8. Religious drama ______________________________.

B) Multiple choice

1. Which of the following structures is probably not an example of a sacred space?

a. Schools
b. Pagodas
c. Churches
d. Pyramids

2. Paul Tillich's definition of religion revolved around what central idea?

a. Belief in a "Beyond".
b. The feeling of awe in the presence of the Holy.
c. The use of symbols and rites.
d. Ultimate concern about the Unconditioned.

3. The wedge-shaped characters used in the ancient writings of Mesopotamia are called

a. Hieroglyphics
b. Cuneiform
c. Letters
d. Kanji

4. Which of the following is true about religious studies?

a. Only committed believers can be scholars of religious studies.
b. Scholars of religious studies try to understand the views of various traditions without judging their truth or falsity.
c. Scholars of religious studies can not participate in any religion.
d. A[illegible]l scholars of religion adopt a "confessional" [illegible]h.

5. Epics can be defined as

a. Sacred stories about what preceded direct human knowledge.
b. Long, narrative poems about feats of heroes.
c. Stories about the beginning of the universe.
d. Movies which deal with religious or spiritual themes.

6. A definition which focuses on how religion works is a

a. Descriptive definition
b. Essential definition
c. Functional definition
d. Normative definition

C) True-False

T F 1. The example of a descriptive definition of religion seems to apply better to the Asian religions than to the religions of Europe.

T F 2. The textbook argues that most religions have a belief in a personal Absolute.

T F 3. In order to maintain their objectivity, it is very important that religious scholars do not believe in any of the world religions.

T F 4. Myths and folk tales will be important for the study of some nonliterate people, but will not be for the study of literate people.

T F 5. Walter Huston Clark believes it is more appropriate to use the concept of "faith" than that of "religion".

T F 6. Rituals are repetitive actions performed as a social obligation.

PART SEVEN ESSAY AND DISCUSSION QUESTIONS

1. Discuss why you are interested in the study of world religions. What issues and topics would you hope to have studied and understood by the end of the semester?

2. While "Religious Studies" or "Religion" is often a separate discipline at many universities and colleges, a scholar of religion will use the methods and techniques of many other disciplines. Try to think of all the different academic disciplines that might enter into the study of Religion. (An example of one such discipline might be Archaeology.) Choose three of these academic disciplines that you have listed. Construct a conversation between three scholars each of whom belong to one of these disciplines. In this conversation have each scholar explain to the others what is the approach of his discipline, and how this approach might be useful to a person attempting to understand world religions. Towards the end of the conversation have the scholars discuss the question of whether using a variety of their approaches would be best for understanding world religions.

3. Why might people who engage in religious studies feel a tension between, on the one hand, maintaining their objectivity and, on the other hand, having empathy for the feelings of religious believers? What are some of the ways one might deal with this tension? How do you see yourself addressing this issue as you study world religion this semester?

4. Compare and contrast the meanings of the term "religion" given by Clark, Tillich and James. What do you think are the strengths and weaknesses of each definition? Why?

PART EIGHT AN ESSAY FOR DEEPER CONSIDERATION

Essay question

At the end of this term you will know much more about religion than you do now. However, it might be interesting for you to think and write about how you view "religion" at the start of your study. You might then want to see if your view of "religion" has changed significantly when you have completed this course. Therefore, write an essay in which you formulate a general definition of "religion". After stating your definition, explain why you believe this to be the most useful definition for understanding different world religions.

Tips for answering:

First, note that you are not being asked to state what you think is the best religion, or the truest religion. Rather, you are being asked to try to come up with a definition of religion that you think will apply to all movements, beliefs or practices that you would consider "religious". You should ask yourself, therefore, whether your definition is too narrow, and applies to only certain types of religions, or certain aspects of religion. But be careful that your definition does not become so broad that it would apply to movements or practices that you would not consider to be "religious" (for example, the Boy Scouts or political parties).

It might be helpful to bear in mind a distinction that many philosophers make when dealing with definitions. Some definitions are what could be termed "definition reports"; that is to say, they attempt to report on how this word or term is actually used by groups of people who speak the language. Dictionaries are the most obvious place to find definition reports. Other definitions, however, are "definition proposals"; an individual proposes to use a word or term in a unique manner in order, perhaps, to isolate the essence of what a word means. The definitions advanced by Clark, Tillich and James in the textbook seem to fall into the category of "definition proposals". In your essay you can make use of both of these types of definitions. For example, you might want to quote and examine dictionary definitions. Notice, however, that the question is asking you to give your own definition proposal, so you probably will only want to use dictionary definitions as a starting point. A proposal need take notice of, but not be limited by, actual usage. Similarly, in your essay you might want to refer to and critique the different proposals mentioned in the text. Just remember that your goal is to formulate your own definition. Such a definition may improve on one of the definitions given in the text, or it might try to combine two of the proposals so as to strengthen the definition.

The text also discusses different types of definitions of religion. In formulating your definition you might want to consider which type of definition you are advancing. What are the strengths of each type of definition? What might be some of the drawbacks to each type of definition?

Finally, the essay question asks that you explain why you believe your definition would be helpful in understanding what is religion. There are a number of ways in which you could approach this task. Notice, for example, how the textbook critiques the proposals by Clark and Tillich; it tries to apply these definitions to actual religious traditions such as Judaism and Buddhism. At this point in your study you might not be familiar with a wide variety of religious traditions. Still, most people do have knowledge of a few different traditions. In your essay you might try to apply your definition to a couple of the religions with which you might be familiar at this time. Do these religious traditions fit with your definition?

PART NINE PROJECTS FOR DEVELOPING RELIGIOUS EMPATHY

1. Many of us have friends or acquaintances who are adherents of different religious traditions, or who were raised in families that believed in other religions. Get together a couple of classmates or friends with backgrounds in religions other than our own. You might want to ask people

from this class, or explain to your friends outside class this is a project for a class. Ask everyone to talk about what religion means to them. What religious tradition did they grow up with, or do they believe in now? What role does religion play in their lives? Do they identify with being a member of a religious group, or do they see religion as more of an individual matter? Ask everyone in the group to try and not judge or evaluate the beliefs of the other people, but to understand and appreciate their beliefs. Share your own background and beliefs.

Notice whether you and the other members of the group can be empathic without judging or trying to convert. What sorts of problems might there be in trying to talk about religion in this way? How might this be relevant to the study of different religions in this class?

2. Increasingly, our society is becoming a multi-religious society. Not only are there usually Roman Catholic and different Protestant denominations in most communities, but often many communities have groups of Jewish, Islamic, Hindu, Buddhist or other religious adherents.

   Get together with a classmate or friend, and by using the Yellow Pages of the telephone directory try and locate a variety of religious group in your town or city. Write down where they have their church, synagogue, temple or mosque. Then take a trip or walk to observe the buildings that house the different religious communities. Where is the building located - in the city, in the country, on a hill? What is the size of the building? What is the shape of the building? How does it use space? Are there any unusual elements or shapes in the building? If so, what might be the reason for including them? Out of what is the building constructed? What appears to be the function or purpose of the building? Do the answers to any of these questions tell you anything about the nature of the religious community or their beliefs or practices? How do the different buildings vary? Are the variations significant, do you think?

3. Go to your college library and try to locate on the shelves a recent textbook for Sociology, Art History, Anthropology and Philosophy. Skim each book to find sections that deal with religion. How does each one deal with religion? What approach does each text seem to take in its study of religion? How do the textbooks differ in how they discuss religion? Do any not deal with religion

at all? Which approach or approaches seem to be most similar to the approach that this class seems likely to adopt? Which ones seem most interesting to you? Why?

ANSWER KEY TO SELF-TEST SECTION

b) Multiple choice

1. a
2. d
3. b
4. b
5. b
6. c

c) True-False

1. F
2. T
3. F
4. F
5. F
6. T

Notes

[1] Peter L. Berger, The Sacred Canopy: Elements of a Sociological Theory of Religion (Garden City, New York: Anchor Books, 1969) 6-7, 8, 19, 25, 27-28.

[2] William James, The Varieties of Religious Experience: A Study in Human Nature (New York: Modern Library, 1902) 29-32.

PART ONE
Religions of Tribes and City-States

PART ONE LEARNING OBJECTIVES

Doing these exercises, in conjunction with reading the textbook, should help you to achieve the following objectives. Read them and see how many you already have mastered; then study the following terms and concepts, and work through the exercises. After you have completed all the exercises, return to this section and review the objectives again.

You should be able to:

1. Define and differentiate between "tribes" and "city-states", and explain briefly some of the characteristics of both "tribal religion" and "city-state religion".

2. Understand the basics of how the size and structure of the group relates to the means of subsistence and the nature of religious beliefs and practices.

PART TWO TERMS AND INDIVIDUALS

A) Terms and Concepts

tribes	tribal religions

city-states
Egyptians
Mesoamerica
myths
immortality
sons of gods
city-state religions
Greeks
iconography
redemption
gods
priests

PART THREE GUIDED REVIEW

1. The two types of religions found in Part I are religions of _______________ and religions of _______________.

2. Smaller tribal groups tend to support themselves through _______________. Religious practices and beliefs are related to this in that ______________________________.

3. Larger tribal groups are organized around _____________. This is connected to religious practices in that _________ ____.

4. City-states are supported by ___________________________. City-state religion focuses on ___________________________.

5. Larger city-states run the danger of __________________.

6. Today, the beliefs and practices of tribal religion is often found alongside ______________________________.

7. Chapters One and Two will study tribal and city-state religions as found in _______________ and _______________.

PART FOUR QUESTIONS FOR CONSIDERATION

As you study the religions of tribes and city-states try to reflect upon, and even write out, responses to the following questions. These questions are designed to help you synthesize what you are learning about the religions of America and Africa, and reach your own conclusions concerning the significance of these traditions.

1. The textbook argues that how a group gains its subsistence can affect its religious beliefs and practices. As you read the next two chapters, decide to which of the size-groups

each of the religions belongs. Can you identify how the group gains its food, how it is organized and what type of religious beliefs and practices these influence? Have any of the groups undergone changes in size and organization? If so, how has the group's religious beliefs and practices changed?

2. After you have studied the religions of North America, Mesoamerica and Africa, try to compare these three families of religions. How strong are the commonalties among religions from the same geographical area? Are the commonalties strong enough to allow us to talk about "families of religions?" Is Egyptian religion so different from the religion of the Zulu, is even the religion of the Basongye so different from the Zulu, that the concept of "African religion" is not very useful?

3. The textbook uses two different schema for talking about the religions in this section. One schema is based on geographical location ("religions of America" vs. "religions of Africa"). The second is based on the size and nature of the society ("tribal religions" vs. "city-state religions".) What is the difference between these two schema? What might be the advantages and disadvantages of each typology? Does one seem to be more useful than the other? Would the use of <u>both</u> be the best approach?

Chapter 1
Religions of The Americas

PART ONE LEARNING OBJECTIVES

Doing these exercises, in conjunction with reading the textbook, should help you to achieve the following objectives. Read them and see how many you already have mastered; then study the following terms and concepts, and work through the exercises. After you have completed all the exercises, return to this section and review the objectives again.

You should be able to:

1. List the manner in which different groups of scholars believe the native people of America migrated to the New World.

2. Discuss the religion of a hunting people, the Naskapi, and demonstrate your knowledge of this religion by using specific examples of their beliefs and practices. In particular, you should be able to delineate the Naskapi beliefs concerning the soul, the hunt and dreams.

3. Discuss the religion of the Kwakiutl people and demonstrate your knowledge of this religion by using specific examples of their beliefs and practices, in particular the potlatch custom.

4. Discuss the religion of an agricultural people, the Powhatan people, and demonstrate your knowledge of this religion by using specific examples of their beliefs and practices. In particular, you should be able to talk and write on the Powhatan views and practices concerning medicine and religion, the gods, and divination and magic.

5. Discuss the religion of a second agricultural people, the Cherokee peoples, and demonstrate your knowledge of this religion by using specific examples of their beliefs and practices. In particular, you should be able to talk and write specifically on the Cherokee worldview stories.

6. Discuss the religion of the Pueblo peoples, the Zuni and the Hopi, and demonstrate your knowledge of this religion by using specific examples of their beliefs and practices. In particular, you should be able to talk and write on the Hopi use of kivas and kachinas.

7. Discuss the religion of the Great Plains people, the Dakota and the Pawnee, and demonstrate your knowledge of this religion by using specific examples of their beliefs and practices. In particular, you should be able to talk and write about the Pawnee Morning Star and Evening Star custom.

8. List and write about some of the common features of religions in North America, including their view of the Absolute, the world, the role of humans, the problem and resolution for humans, community and ethics, and their relations with other religions.

9. Discuss and analyze the Aztec religion, including being able to discuss the Aztec view of the gods, and man's relationship to the gods. You should also be able to describe the major Aztec rituals.

10. Discuss and analyze the religion of the Incas, including being able to discuss the Inca beliefs in the gods and other manifestations such as the huacas and to describe at least one major Inca religious ritual.

11. Analyze what roles dreams can play in religion, and illustrate that you know Freud's and Jung's basic theories of dream interpretation.

PART TWO TERMS AND INDIVIDUALS

A) Terms and Concepts

RELIGIONS OF NORTH AMERICA

the Naskapi people
shaman
Tsaka'bec
Caribou Man
Kwakiutl people
Potlatch
Powhatan Peoples
weroances
weroansquas
Ahone
Pocahontas
Cherokees
Pueblo Peoples
Awonawilona
kivas
Peoples of the Great Plain
Wakan tanka
Morning Star/Evening Star
monotheism
Native American Church
mantu
Mista'peo
trickster
reincarnation
totems
totem poles
mamanatowick
wisakon
Okeus
huskanaw
Powhatan
myth
Zuni
Hopi
kachinas
Dakota people
Pawnee
human sacrifice
henotheism

AZTECS

Tenochtitlan
Chichimec
Tlaloc
Xochiquetzal
Tezcatlipoca
Quetzalcoatl
Hernando Cortez
Huitzilopochtli
Coatlicue
Tlazolteotl
Tonatiuh
The Stone of the Sun
Aztecs

INCAS

Cuzco
Inti
huacas
Situa
huayaya
Coriancha
Viracocha
virgins of the sun
yahuar sanco
Archetypes

B) Individuals and Terms from Other Traditions

Christianity
Sigmund Freud
C. G. Jung
Joseph Campbell

PART THREE GUIDED REVIEW

1. The three theories by scholars concerning the settling of South America by its native people are ________________, ________________, and ______________________.

2. The textbook divides Religions of the Americas into two parts: the Religion of ______________________ and the Religion of ___________________________.

3. The textbook classifies the religion of the Naskapi people as a religion of ____________.

4. The Naskapi may not have converted to Christianity because they believe that their ancient religion, unlike Christianity, can help them ___________________.

5. The Naskapi believe that stars, fish, trees and humans are all filled with __________ or, in their language, __________.

6. A shaman is defined as ________________________.

7. The essential person, who is located in the heart and is the active soul of each person, is called the _______________.

8. The figure in myths who is able to use his wits and cleverness to achieve his ends is called by scholars a ____________.

9. While the Naskapi believe that using the proper hunting tools and having hunting skills are relevant to a successful hunt, even more important is ___________________________. This often occurs in ___________.

10. The Kwatiutl people are famous for their totems, which are ___________________, and for their potlatch, which means __________________________.

11. A major difference between the Naskapi and the Powhatan peoples is that the Powhaten ____________________________.

12. The great king who ruled the Powhatan people was called a ________________, and he ruled his area through the _______________, who were _________________________.

13. According to the Powhatan, two activities that were grouped together were _____________ and _____________.

14. The Powhatan believed in a good god, _____________. Even more attention was given to the deity of ill-will, ____________. The reason for giving more attention to the latter may be because the Powhatan wanted to ____.

15. The English believed that during the huskanaw ceremony what occurred was __________________________. However, some modern scholars now believe that what occurred was actually ____.

16. Much of the religion of the Cherokees revolved around ________________, which were open only to _________________.

17. The Cherokees explain the creation of the earth in the following manner: ____ ____.

18. Animals such as the panther and the owl can see at night because ____.

19. The Cherokees believe that today they have to hunt for game because at one time _______________________________________.

20. The story of the "corn woman" is shared by the Cherokees and other native American peoples; it is the story of a woman who can ____.

21. In the sacred stories of the Zuni people, Awonawilona is a ____.

22. The traditional, doll-like figures used by the Hopi people are called ________________________________.

23. Buffalo, bear, the four winds and the whirlwind were for the Dakota __________________________________.

24. One disturbing ritual practiced by the Pawnee was that of ____.

25. Most religions of North America had a ______________ view of the Absolute, not a ___________________ view.

26. Among religions of North America a belief in a good creator spirit was often offset by the belief in __________.

27. Many of the religions of North America see the relation between animals and humans as being one of ______________. To illustrate this they believe that _________________________.

28. Two explanations in the religious beliefs of native Americans for the suffering and problems faced by humans are ________________________ and ____________________________.

29. Three ways in which native Americans used healing in their beliefs and practices were _______________________, _______________________, and _________________________.

30. For native Americans time was usually viewed as _______________.

31. Native American rituals for the dead include ___________, ____________________, and ______________________.

32. The chief deity of the Aztecs was Huitzilopochtli, the god of _____________. The Aztecs believed that he needed to be fed ____.

33. The female goddesses of the Aztecs symbolized the powers of ____.

34. The Stone of the Sun could be described as _____________ ____. It symbolized ____.

35. Since it was believed that the sun could only be kept alive with sufficient supplies of blood, the Aztecs held that human life depended on ________________________________.

36. The heart of the Inca Empire was located in __________ ____________________________.

37. The chief of the Incas was the representative of ___________________. The Coricancha was __________________ ______________________.

38. The early god of the Incas was ____________. He was symbolized by ___________________ carried by the priests in a basket.

39. This earlier god was superseded by _______________, who, it was believed, created ____________________________.

40. Unusual appearances in rocks or plants, or the city of Cuzco itself, were termed ____________ and were seen by the Incas as ____________________.

41. The Situa festival involved three stages:
a)____,
b)____,
and c) ____.

42. One common feature of the city-state religions of Mesoamerica and South America was that _____________, _________________ and _________________ were seen as interdependent.

43. The problem for a human being in these city-state societies was to ____.
This was done by ____.

44. The belief that dreams can be used to reveal the truth is not limited to the cultures of included in this chapter; among thinkers of the Twentieth Century who believed dreams could be used to reveal the truth about the human condition were ______________ and ______________.

45. The figures and themes that Jung believed were common to the dreams of all people are called ______________________.

PART FOUR ANALYZING TEXTS

In most of the subsequent chapter of this study guide you will be asked to read and analyze scriptures taken from the religious traditions discussed in that particular chapter. These texts have been chosen precisely because they contain ideas and concepts with which you should be familiar after reading the textbook and studying the actual writings of the various traditions. In the case of this chapter this approach is very difficult. Most of the tribes or people studied in this chapter did not write down their beliefs or stories. However, the textbook does describe the beliefs and practices of a number of these peoples. Running through these descriptions are a number of shared characteristics; characteristics that the textbook helps to isolate.

Below are three passages written by famous scholars of religion. Each passage deals with one aspects of religious expression, an aspect which is important in the religious expressions of peoples of the Americas. Read each passage carefully, and try to analyze it by addressing the following questions: Upon what aspect of religion does the passage focus? What examples of this function or idea can you find in the religions discussed in the textbook? Do the examples provided in the textbook support the position taken in the passage, or do they support a different position? Does the textbook provide examples of scholars of religion who have taken different views of this subject? This analysis may also help to sharpen your define of "religion".

TEXT ONE

> Let us consider the deepest and most fundamental element in all strong and sincerely felt religious emotion. . . If we do so we shall find we are dealing with something for which there is only one appropriate expression, "*mysterium tremendum*". The feeling of it may at times come sweeping like a gentle tide, pervading the mind with a tranquil mood of deepest worship. It may pass over into a more set and lasting attitude of the soul, continuing, as it were, thrillingly vibrant and resonant, until at last it dies away and the soul resumes its "profane," non-religious mood of everyday experience. It may burst in sudden eruption up from the depths of the soul with spasms and convulsions, or lead to the strangest excitements, to intoxicated frenzy, to transport, and to ecstasy. . . . Conceptually *mysterium* denotes merely that which is hidden and esoteric, that which is beyond conception of understanding, extraordinary and unfamiliar. . . . *Tremor* is in itself merely the perfectly familiar and "natural" emotion of *fear*. But here the term is taken, aptly enough but still only by analogy, to denote a quite specific kind of emotional response, wholly distinct from that of being afraid, though it so far resembles it that the analogy of fear may be used to throw light upon its nature. . . To "keep a thing holy in the heart" means to mark it off by a feeling of peculiar dread, not to be mistaken for any ordinary dread . . . [1]

TEXT TWO

It is now possible to approach the main distinction between myths and folktales, a source of unbounded confusion in nearly all discussion of myths. Is it really feasible to separate the two? . . . I would offer a preliminary and incomplete definition of folktales, independently of their association with any type of society or level of culture, as follows: they are traditional tales, of no firmly established form, in which supernatural elements are subsidiary; they are not primarily concerned with 'serious' subjects or the reflexion of deep problems and preoccupations; and their first appeal lies in their narrative interest. . . What are usually termed 'myths" . . . tend to behave differently. The characters, particularly the hero, are specific, and their family relationships are carefully noted . . . The action is complicated, and often broken up into loosely related episodes. It does not usually depend on disguises and tricks, but rather on the unpredictable reactions of individuals, personalities rather than types. Indeed one of the distinguishing characteristics of myths is their free-ranging and often paradoxical fantasy. . . In addition, myths tend to possess that element of 'seriousness', in establishing and confirming rights and institutions or exploring and reflecting problems or preoccupations . . . For myths, specific though they may be in their characters and local settings, are usually envisaged as taking place in a timeless past. . . The action of folktales, on the other hand, is assumed to have taken place within historical time, in the past often enough, but not the distant or primeval past.[2]

TEXT THREE

The most elementary forms of behavior motivated by religious or magical factors are oriented to this world. Even human sacrifices, uncommon among urban peoples, were performed in the Phoenician maritime cities without any otherworldly expectations whatsoever. Furthermore, religiously or magically motivated behavior is relatively rational behavior, especially in its earliest manifestations. It follows rules of experience, though it is not necessarily action in accordance with a means-end schema. Rubbing will elicit sparks from pieces of wood, and in like fashion the simulative actions of a

> magician will evoke rain from the heavens. . . . . Thus, religious or magical behavior or thinking must not be set apart from the range of everyday purposive conduct, particularly since even the ends of the religious and magical actions are predominantly economic.[3]

PART FIVE SELF-TEST

A) <u>Definitions and Descriptions</u> - Write your own definition or description of each of the following terms. After completing the self-test, check your answer with the definition or description given in the textbook.

1. Okeus ____
____
____.

2. huskanaw ____
____
____.

3. Quetzalcoatl ____
____
____.

4. archetypes (C. G. Jung) ____
____
____.

5. weroances ____
____
____.

6. Mista'peo ____
____
____.

7. shaman ____
____
____.

8. Morning Star/Evening Star ____
____
____.

9. huacas ____
____
____.

10. trickster____
____
____.

B) Multiple choice

1. Which of the following peoples is mentioned in this chapter as a nonliterate, hunting people?

   a. Cherokees
   b. Naskapi
   c. Hebrews
   d. Powhatan

2. The chief god of the Aztecs was

   a. Huitzilopochtli.
   b. Tlaloc.
   c. Tonatiuh.
   d. Tezcatlipoca.

3. Which of the following would it be incorrect to say about Tsaka'bec?

   a. He is the man in the moon.
   b. He is a trickster.
   c. He is the Caribou Man.
   d. He is a central figure in the Naskapi myths.

4. The Potlatch custom of the Kwakiutl People can be defined as

   a. Ancestor-like figures of clans
   b. Dream predictions by shamans
   c. Hosts giving away as much wealth as possible
   d. Human sacrifice of a young maiden

5. Which of the following historical figures is not mentioned as having studied the significance of dreams?

   a. C. G. Jung
   b. Rudolph Otto
   c. Sigmund Freud
   d. Joseph Campbell

6. According to the Naskapi people the world is filled with

   a. mamanatowick
   b. mista'peo
   c. mantu
   d. myth

7. Which of the following is <u>not</u> one of the acts of the Inca Situa festival?

   a. The Emperor orders the city purged of all foreign influences.
   b. Inca knights go to battle throughout the city.
   c. Participants eat or wear a kind of dough.
   d. The emperor is sacrificed to the sun god in order to ensure a good harvest.

8. The greatest difference between the religions of most of the peoples in this chapter, and major world religions is that

   a. Major world religions do not make use of myths.
   b. Major world religions write about their beliefs.
   c. The religions in this chapter use dream interpretation.
   d. The religions in this chapter were developed in city-states.

9. The Powhatan people classified religion together with

   a. witchcraft
   b. agriculture
   c. law
   d. medicine

10. Which of the following stories is <u>not</u> mentioned as one of the Cherokee myths?

   a. The story of how the flood covered the earth.
   b. The story of how the earth was created.
   c. The story of how the first human was born.
   d. The story of why Indians must hunt.

C) <u>True-False</u>

T F 1. An archetype can be defined as the appearance in dreams of the material of the Id repressed by the Superego.

T F 2. The Cherokees had a myth about the corn woman, who produced corn by rubbing her stomach.

T F 3. The Aztecs sacrificed many people because they believed the blood and hearts of the victims kept the sun alive.

T F 4. A few scholars believe that the west coast of South America may have been settled by people sailing from Pacific islands.

T F 5. The Powhatan Indians kept the bodies of their dead commanders in loaf-shaped temples.

T F 6. The view of the Absolute in religions of native people of North America can best be described as <u>monotheistic</u> rather than as <u>henotheistic</u>.

T F 7. In some religions of North America the initiation ritual for young men could result in injury or even death.

T F 8. The most important myth for the Naskapi people is their creation myth.

T F 9. The Naskapi people believe that communication with the souls of animals is more important than the skill of the hunter.

T F 10. For many nonliterate people the role of the good gods may not be as important as that of malevolent deities or spirits.

PART SIX ESSAY AND DISCUSSION QUESTIONS

1. Describe what you believe are the most important qualities and characteristics that distinguish religions of North America from those of Semitic or Asian origin? What do these characteristics tell us about the nature of religion among nonliterate people?

2. Compare and contrast the religion of a hunting people to

the religion of an agricultural people, choosing one agricultural and one hunting culture from those you have studied in the textbook. What are the differences and the similarities in the beliefs, myths, and rituals of the two peoples?

3. "Power" plays an important role in many of the religions described in this chapter; power over the hunt, over other people, over shamans or witches. How might you define "power" in the context of the religions studied in this chapter? What role does "power" play in the religions of nonliterate cultures? Why might cultures such as those discussed here be concerned with power?

4. Explain Freud's and Jung's theories concerning dreams. Do the theories of either man help us to understand dreams and their role in the religions of nonliterate people?

5. Explain how the Aztecs viewed the universe, man's role in the universe, and his relation with the gods.

6. Describe how the Absolute might be manifest in the day to day life of the Incas.

7. Delineate, in your own words, the basic features of both religions of nonliterate people, and city-state religion. How would you compare these two types of religions?

PART SEVEN CONFRONTING QUESTIONS AND ISSUES

Many of the elements found in the religions of nonliterate peoples such as those of North America are also present in the major world religions. Almost all religious traditions have included within themselves myths, the use of magical practices and the interpretation of dreams. And yet, how relevant are such elements for religion in the modern age? Given advances in the fields of history, science and psychology, can, and should, religions continue to employ myths, magic and dreams? Are such elements an important and necessary part of religious experience? Or are they the outdated heritage of the nonliterate, non-rational religions of the past?

By considering the following problem you might uncover your views on religion for modern man. Choose a religious tradition with which you are familiar. It may be, if you wish, a tradition in which you actually believe and participate. Or it may be one which you have studied, perhaps one of the traditions you read about in this chapter. Imagine, in either case, that you are an active participant in this tradition. One night you have a dream which could be interpreted as having religious significance. Perhaps a famous religious figure from history appears in the dream, giving you a message. Or maybe the dream contains a message on how to live your life according to the values of this tradition. Or maybe you can use a dream that you have actually had in the past few nights.

Once you have chosen a dream, consider what interpretation you would give to this dream. Would you see it as having religious or spiritual significance and make changes in your life because of the dream? Or would you interpret the dream in a non-religious manner? In either case, why would you choose this approach to the dream? What does your position concerning the significance of the dream tell you about your view of religion's role in the modern age? Is it possible for you, living in the Twentieth Century, to view dreams, in the manner of the Naskapi, as religious messages? Why or why not?

PART EIGHT AN ESSAY FOR DEEPER CONSIDERATION

Essay Question

Describe, in your own words, one of the myths discussed in this chapter. Also explain what function it may perform in the society from which it comes.

Tips For Answering

In subsequent chapters of this study guide you will be asked to write on more complex essay questions. This question asks you to develop your essay along somewhat simpler lines, but is still complex enough to challenge one's writing and analytical skills, and to benefit from a brief analysis.

This essay question is basically asking you to give a description, or, actually, two descriptions. A description of something might be defined as giving in words an account of the nature, or appearance, or key points, or function of that thing. First, the question is asking you to describe a myth from a one of the religions of the Americas. Second, it is asking you to describe the myth's function in the society. The first type of description is the simpler of the two.

You are being asked to choose and describe one of the myths you have studied. This description will be essentially a retelling of that myth. In all but very unusual cases your description of this myth will not be based on work in the field, but on the description of the myth given in the textbook. What you will be doing, therefore, is paraphrasing the description given in the textbook. While rhetoricians differ in their exact definitions of "paraphrasing", the following seems to express the essence of a paraphrase. It is to restate in your own words the ideas of another that are contained in a short passage. An important point to remember is that you must make the way in which you convey these ideas, not just the words, your own. So, in describing the myth you choose, you should convey the same story, but do so in a way that does not duplicate the textbook and is distinctively your own.

The second part of the question is asking you to describe the myth's function in society: why is this particular myth important for this society and what role does it play in this society? This type of description might be termed an "analytical description." It is not just asking you to retell the story, but to go further and give an account of how these nonliterate people make use of the myth so your reader can understand both the myth and the society. In order to do this you might consider describing the nature of the society, and how this myth is appropriate for such a society. Or you might look at the structure of the society, and see if this structure is reflected in the myth.

PART NINE PROJECTS FOR DEVELOPING RELIGIOUS EMPATHY

1. This chapter discusses the important role that dreams play in the religions of many nonliterate peoples. In cultures such as that of the Naskapi, dreams are used to predict the future or teach the hunter. Today, we often look to dreams not to predict the future, but to reveal aspects of ourselves normally hidden from our conscious minds. But our dreams may also be a door through which we can gain entry into the consciousness of earlier, nonliterate peoples, and develop empathy for their way of life. As Jung stated:

> One cannot afford to be naive in dealing with dreams. They originate in a spirit that is not quite human, but is rather a breath of nature - a spirit of the beautiful and generous as well as of the cruel goddess. If we want to characterize this spirit, we shall certainly get closer to it in the sphere of ancient mythologies, or the fables of the primeval forest, than in the consciousness of modern man.[4]

To get in touch with this primeval spirit, and to understand the role that dreams have played in nonliterate cultures, you might want to keep a dream journal. Such a journal is easy to begin, but it does require some discipline and preparation. First, you should put a notebook and a pen by the side of your bed, where you can easily reach it. You will want to write down your dreams as soon as you awake. Next, every night before you fall asleep, tell yourself that you will remember at least one dream and will write it down. Repeat this to yourself a number of times. Then, when you wake up in the night or in the morning, get in the habit of immediately writing down whatever you can remember of your dreams. This is important, since waiting even one or two minutes can result in much of the dream being forgotten. Just write down everything you can remember. Finally, later in the day or evening, reread the description and jot down any thoughts or reflections you have on the dream. Why might you have dreamt what you did? Could your dream be a reflection of any events or concerns in your life? How might a person from one of the cultures in this chapter have interpreted your dream? Would you accept this interpretation? Why or why not?

2. The author of the textbook states that myths are not to be found only in ancient religions, but also in contemporary life. Try to think of examples of myths that we Americans believe in or use. You might first want to review the different definitions or theories of myths presented in the textbook, in order to help you decide what is and is not a myth. Lauri Hanko suggests four criteria for myths: a) it tells a story of origin or creation, b) talks about the beginning of time, c) it sets a model for behavior and d) it is tied to a ritual. Is this analysis useful? Using the definition you choose, what examples of myths can you find? Are any of these myths actually stories of "gods"? How many of the myths are related to stories of the beginnings of our country, and the form of our

government? How many relate to our jobs or careers? In what way do these myths contribute to the self-image we have as Americans? Do you think we are aware of these as myths, or are myths only myths when we do not consciously question them?

3. Story-telling appears to be making a comeback in our culture. At day-care centers and at open-air festivals, one can find story-tellers practicing their art. Many ethnic groups are promoting story-telling as a way to hand on their heritage to future generations. Even on the radio, story-tellers such as Garrison Keillor or "Rabbit Ears Radio" are attracting new audiences.

   Among nonliterate societies story-telling is crucial. Cultures which lack a written language must pass on their stories by telling them orally, and must develop ways to do so with great accuracy. However, in telling and re-telling the story, each teller shapes the story by his skill and to his needs. As G. S. Kirk has argued:

   > Every time a poem or a tale is sung or recited, unless there is a written version - or in rare cases an oral one so sacrosanct that it is known virtually by heart - its form is slightly altered. . . . [This] is a generalization that seems valid wherever it can be checked among non-literate societies, whether primitive or not, and one which seems to accord with several distinct human capacities and limitations. . . they will be varied in some degree on virtually every occasion of telling, and the variations will be determined by the whim, the ambition or the particular thematic repertoire of the individual teller, as well as by the receptivity and special requirements of the particular audience.[5]

   Listen to friends who you might consider to be good story-tellers as they spin their tales. What sort of stories do they tell? How do they structure their stories to keep the audiences interest? When you hear them tell the same story a number of times, how do they change the tale? Do they alter the story according to the audience? Do these observations give you any insights into the role of story-telling in a culture without a written language (or even more important without television or multi-media technology?)

ANSWER KEY TO SELF-TEST

b) Multiple choice

1. b
2. a
3. c
4. c
5. b
6. c
7. d
8. b
9. d
10. a

c) True-False

1. F
2. T
3. T
4. T
5. T
6. F
7. T
8. F
9. T
10. T

Notes

[1]Rudolf Otto, The Idea of the Holy, 2nd ed., trans. John W. Harvey, (Oxford: Oxford University Press, 1950) 12-14.

[2]G. S. Kirk, Myth: Its Meaning and Functions in Ancient and Other Cultures (Berkeley: University of California Press, 1973) 34-40.

[3]Max Weber, The Sociology of Religion, 4th ed. trans. Ephraim Fischoff (1922; Boston: Beacon Press, 1964) 1.

[4]Carl Jung, "Approaching the Unconscious," Man and His Symbols, ed. Jung and M.L. von Franz (Garden City, NY: Doubleday, 1964).

[5]G. S. Kirk, Myth: Its Meaning and Functions in Ancient and Other Cultures (Berkeley, CA: University of California Press, 1973) 73-74.

Chapter 2
Religions of Africa

PART ONE LEARNING OBJECTIVES

Doing these exercises, in conjunction with reading the textbook, should help you to achieve many of the following objectives. Read them and see how many you already have mastered; then study the following terms and concepts, and work through the exercises. After you have completed all the exercises, review the objectives again.

You should be able to:

1. Understand the scope of human habitation in Africa.

2. Know and write down a brief outline of ancient Egyptian history, and how this history was reflected in Egyptian religious beliefs and practices.

3. Describe the nature and characteristics of Egyptian religion, including being able to describe the major Egyptian deities, some Egyptian religious practices, and Egyptian views of the Absolute, and of life after death.

4. Cite some examples of how Egyptian religion influenced the beliefs and practices of other cultures.

5. Discuss the religion of the Basongye of Zaire, and demonstrate your knowledge of their religion by referring to specific examples of their beliefs and practices. In

particular, you should be able to talk and write about the Basongye belief in and use of magic.

6. Discuss the religion of the Zulu peoples, and demonstrate your knowledge of their religion by referring to specific examples of their beliefs and practices. In particular, you should be able to talk and write about Zulu beliefs concerning the ancestors, the role of religious functionaries, rites of passage and the deities.

7. Discuss the religion of the Yoruba peoples, and demonstrate your knowledge of their religion by referring to specific examples of their beliefs and practices. In particular, you should be able to talk and write about Yoruba beliefs concerning the various deities, the human role in the world, and the role of religious functionaries and festivals.

8. Discuss and analyze some of the common features of the religions in Sub-Saharan Africa, including the beliefs about the Absolute, the world, the human role, the problem and solution for humans, rituals and symbols, and life after death.

9. Define the concept of "divination", explain the role of divination in African religion, and give examples of the importance of divination in religious traditions from other cultures.

PART TWO TERMS AND INDIVIDUALS

A) Terms and Concepts

Homo erectus
Homo sapiens
Homo sapiens afer
Homo sapiens rhodesiensis
Bushmanoid
Pygmoid
Negroid
Caucasoid
Niger-Kordofanian
Nilo-Saharan
Hamito-Semitic
Khosian
Austronesian
Arabic

EGYPT

pyramid
hieroglyphics
Old Kingdom
First Intermediate Period

Middle Kingdom
Early New Kingdom
Armarna Revolution
Horus
Osiris
Aton
Mayet (Maat)
Bast
Seth
ba

Second Intermediate Period
Later New Kingdom
Hyksos
Isis
Amon-Re (Ra)
Hathor
Sakhmet
ankh
ka
akh (ikhu)

SUB-SAHARAN AFRICA

Bantus
Efile Mukulu
buchi
mankishi
Zulu people
Umnumzane
diviner (isangoma)
izinyanga zezulu
ancestors
ukubuyisa idlozi
Inkosazana
Inkosi Yezulu
Yoruba people
Ibo people
aworo
olori ebi
Olorun
Gelede festival
ase
Agemo
Orun (Olodumare)
omoraiye
Odudwa
oloogun
Nuer people
masks
infibulation
abiku

Basongye people
Kafilefile
kikudu
mikishi
kraals
umsamo
izinyanga zemithi
abathakati
ihlambo
u mueling angi
umnayama
ubuthongo
Hausa people
orisha-nla
Orunmila
oba
Esu
awon iya wa
orisha
ori inun
Aiye
Obatala
elegun
egungun
Dinka people
clitoridectomy
babalawo

B) Individuals

EGYPT

Pharaoh Cheops
Queen Hatshepsut

Pharaoh Akhenaton

SUB-SAHARAN AFRICA

Patrice Lumumba
Nelson Mandela

C) Texts

Egyptian Book of the Dead

D) Individuals and Terms From Other Traditions

Christianity
Nubians
Ptolemies
Mark Antony
Maimonides
Hinduism
Jesus
I Ching
Islam
Hyksos
Byzantine empire
Julius Caesar
King Leopold of Belgium
Judaism
Muhammad

PART THREE GUIDED REVIEW

1. Remains of homo sapiens have been found in Africa dating back to at least _________.

2. Whereas a "city-state" refers to ______________________________ ____________________, the term "tribe" refers to __________ ___________________________________.

3. One major difference between Egyptian religion and the religions of Sub-Saharan Africa discussed in the textbook is that Egyptian religion could be classified as a ____________ religion, whereas the religions of such groups as the Zulu and the Basongye could be classified as _______________ religions.

4. If one looks at Africa today, the Basongye are to found in the country of ______________, the Zulu in ________________, and the Yoruba in ________________.

5. The earliest Egyptian civilization began along __________ ____________________.

6. The writing system used by the Egyptians is called ______________________, which could be described as _________ ____.

7. The king of the gods for the Egyptians was ____________, who was symbolized by a _______________.

8. The goddess who was symbolized by a woman's body with the head of a cow was called ________________. She was the _____________________________.

9. The unity of the Egyptian worldview emphasized an important aspect of life in Egypt: ____________________.

10.The Egyptian temple represented ______________________. Among the duties of the priests at a temple might be to _______________________, to _________________, and to _____________________________.

11. For the Egyptians, Osiris symbolized ____________________ ____.

12. The soul for the Egyptians was comprised of the ________, the _____________, and the akh or ikhu. The akh could be defined as ____.

13. The process that bound together the ka and the body is called ______________________________.

14. After one died, one would appear for judgment before __________________.

15. King Amenhotep IV is noted for _______________________. This change was reversed by his son, _____________________.

16. The Egyptians preserved the human body after death in an attempt to ________________________________.

17. While the Basongye people believe in gods, their religion is much more concerned, for example, with ___________________ and ____________________________.

18. For the people of the village of Lupupa Ngye, the most essential part of a human is his _______________________.

19. If a Lupupan couple wanted to have a child, they might very well employ a ________________________.

20. Every aspect of the daily lives of the Basongye people is influenced by ____________. Among the people one might find engaging in this practice are _________________ and ________________________.

21. The Zulu people traditionally live in a circle of houses termed a ______________. The house of the headman/priest is called a ______________. In this house is a ____________.

22. Three other Zulu religious functionaries are ___________, ____________, and _______________.

23. A Zulu boy is given his first milk from a cow because ____.

24. Rituals such as the ihlambo and ukubuyisa idlozi ceremonies are designed to ______________________________.

25. Inkosazana is __________________, and protects ____.

26. The basic unit of religion among the Yoruba people is the ________________, which is headed by the __________________.

27. Rather than directly approaching Olorun, the primary power of the sky, one approaches him indirectly through the ___________________.

28. The tribes from sub-Saharan Africa examined in the textbook believe that the world is filled with ____.

29. The Zulu and Yoruba believe that each person has his or her ________________________. A person can rediscover this through ____________________.

30. William Bascom argues that the babalawo is a focal point in Yoruba religion because he ______________________________ ____.

PART FOUR ANALYZING TEXTS

Below is a religious text that was not in the textbook. It does, however, contain ideas and concepts with which you should be familiar after reading the textbook and studying the selections in the textbook from primary religious documents. Read it carefully, and try to analyze it by answering the following questions: What are the main ideas in the text? What viewpoint or viewpoints might the author of the text represent? Is it possible to identify the specific thinker, discipline, movement, tradition or work from which the text derives? What intellectual, literary, social, cultural or historical influences are reflected in the text? For each of your conclusions, try to point to specific evidence in the text (e.g. terms, ideas, arguments, writing style, etc.) which supports your conclusion. Be careful that your conclusions do not exceed the evidence upon which they rest.

TEXT ONE

How manifold are thy works!
They are hidden before men,
O sole God, beside whom there is no other.
Thou didst create the earth according to thy heart.

Thou didst make the distant sky in order to rise
therein,
In order to behold all that thou hast made . . .
The world subsists in thy hand,
Even as thou hast made them.

When thou hast risen they live,
When thou settest they die;
For thou art length of life of thyself,
Men live through thee.[1]

PART FIVE SELF-TEST

A) Definitions and Descriptions - Write your own definition or description of each of the following terms. After completing the self-test, check your answer with the definition or description given in the textbook.

1. city-states ________________________________
____
____.

2. Amon-Re ____________________________________
____
____.

3. ba ____
____
____.

4. Efile Mukulu ____
____
____.

5. mikishi ____
____
____.

6. Aton ____
____
____.

7. Orun ____
____
____.

8. Ihlambo ____
____
____.

9. Middle Kingdom ____
____
____.

10. Umsamo ____
____
____.

B) Multiple Choice

1. If a Lupapan couple wanted to make sure they had a child, they probably would

   a. Use a small carved figure.
   b. Consult with a shaman over the meaning of their dreams.
   c. Pray to Efile Mukulu.
   d. Pray to Kafilefile.

2. The Egyptian leader who appears to have worshiped only one god was

   a. King Tutankhamen.
   b. King Cheops.
   c. King Akhenaton.
   d. King Vidor.

3. Mummification for the Egyptians was supposed to bind the body to what aspect of the soul?

   a. ba
   b. ikhu
   c. akh
   d. ka

4. The ceremony among the Zulu known as the ihlambo means

   a. being brought home
   b. herding the sheep
   c. washing the spears
   d. trance of deep-sleep

5. Among the Yoruba the god of Ife who began creation is

   a. Olori ebi
   b. Oba
   c. Orisha
   d. Odudwa

6. The specialist in medicine among the Yoruba is the

   a. egungun
   b. oloogun
   c. elegun
   d. oba

7. The famous pyramid of Cheops was built in the

   a. Old Kingdom Period
   b. Middle Kingdom Period
   c. Second Intermediate Period
   d. Later New Kingdom Period

8. In the very important Egyptian myth of Isis and Osiris, their son who was symbolized by a falcon was

   a. Hathor.
   b. Horus.
   c. Aton.
   d. Seth.

9. A person in Zulu society who uses spiritual forces for evil ends is termed a

   a. abathakati
   b. babalawo
   c. umnumzane
   d. esu

10. Which of the following would be considered a religion of an ancient city-state?

   a. The religion of the Zulu
   b. The religion of the Egyptians
   c. The religion of the Yoruba
   d. The religion of the Basongye

C) <u>True-False</u>

T F 1. In the Egyptian religion, when the god Mayet went to judge you and weighed your heart in a balance, the lighter your heart, the better you had been in life.

T F 2. The Basongye religion believes that the person is composed of his body and his shadow, but do not have any notion of a spirit or soul.

T F 3. An animal who was accorded great honor in Egypt was the cat.

T F 4. The notion of a city-state would apply to the Basongye and the Zulu people.

T F 5. The writing system that the ancient Egyptians used is called cuneiform.

T F 6. Among the Zulu diviners could often be women.

T F 7. Ancestors are very important in the religious traditions of both the Zulu and the Yoruba.

T F 8. The agricultural cycle was associated with the events in the lives of Isis and Osiris.

T F 9. Akhenaton lived during the Old Kingdom Period.

T F 10. For many tribal religions the role of the good gods may not be as important as that of malevolent deities or spirits.

PART SIX ESSAY AND DISCUSSION QUESTIONS

1. What is distinctive in the religious beliefs and practices of the ancient Egyptians?

2. Imagine that by some miracle of time travel you could actually live in ancient Egypt during the Old Kingdom Period. What would be the differences in how this society saw man, his place in the universe and his relation to the gods compared to how American society of today sees these aspects? In which society would you prefer to live? Why?

3. Both the Mesopotamian myths (which are discussed in Chapter Seven of the textbook) and the Greek myths deal with the actions of the gods and how these actions affect human life. To what extent, and in what specific ways, do the myths from the two traditions attempt to justify for humans the actions and ways of the gods?

4. Delineate, in your own words, the basic features of both the religions of Sub-Saharan Africa and that of the Kingdoms of Egypt. How would you compare these two types of religion? What are some of the convergencies between them? What are some of the divergences?

5. What role does magic play in the religions of sub-Saharan Africa? How would you define "magic", and what is its relation to religion?

6. Divination plays a major role in many traditional African religions. In an essay critically examine the statement of Bascom's that divination, for the Yoruba, helps the people deal with a range of personalized and impersonal forces, and helps them achieve their individual destinies.

PART SEVEN CONFRONTING QUESTIONS AND ISSUES

The religion of ancient Egypt has today ceased to be a "live option", to use William James's phrase, for most of us. This ancient faith has long ago been supplanted by Islam, Christianity or a modern faith in man himself. And yet, as the chapter in the textbook made clear, Egyptian religion has had an important influence on more contemporary world religions and on Western culture. In many senses, this is one of the roots of our heritage. Scholars continue to study Egyptian culture and religion, uncovering in the sands of time and the sands of the desert new clues on what the Egyptians believed. These scholars, however, must try to understand not only individual facts concerning ancient Egypt, but also a "worldview" or a "universe of discourse" that seems very different from our own. In the same way the belief of the Basongye in "magic" and "witches" may not seem like a "live option" to many people. Such beliefs often strike many in the West as "irrational." Yet, for the people within that tradition these beliefs very much make "sense." The problem is to know how to understand and "get inside" their sensible world.

It is often easier to discover new texts or monuments from one of these ancient city-states or different cultures, than to understand the consciousness that lies behind the artifact. Many of the rituals from these cultures, and the beliefs that underlie the rituals, appear to us as irrational. When, for example, you read in the first chapter of the textbook that the Aztecs killed many humans every day in order to feed their blood and hearts to Huitzilopochtli, you may feel horror and revulsion. But you may also feel that their belief that this must be done in order to make sure that the sun rises everyday lacks any kind of mental clarity or well thought out order. Such beliefs do not "make sense" to us. Nevertheless, it is too easy to dismiss the Aztec worldview as totally irrational. These beliefs must have made some sort of "sense" to the Aztecs, for they oriented their lives around them. In addition, part of the task of a scholar of religion is to discover and communicate the order that lies beneath such beliefs.

Imagine, then, that you are a scholar studying an ancient city-state religion. Assume for the moment that you are studying the Egyptians or the Basongye. How you would deal with the following questions, and how your answers to these questions might influence your study and be influenced by your study: How is it possible for you, a person of the

Twentieth century living in the United States, to understand a way of living and thinking such as that of the Basongye or the ancient Egyptians? Does such a way of thinking possess a type of reason or order, or is it merely an irrational type of thought? If it does possess a sort of rationality, is there a difference between the way the Basongye, for example, look at and order their world and the way we look at and order our world? What might be some of the methods that scholars of religion use to bridge such gaps between cultures? Is the gap greater or lesser in the case of the Basongye than in the case of the world of Jesus of Nazareth, or Gautama Buddha? Can it be that some cultures will be closed forever to our understanding?

Recently, many philosophers have examined the question of rationality and culture. Among the most provocative has been Peter Winch. One article you might want to consult is his "The Idea of a Social Science", which can be found in an excellent collection of papers on this subject entitled _Rationality_, edited by Bryan Wilson.

PART EIGHT AN ESSAY FOR DEEPER CONSIDERATION

Essay Question

Compare the view of the after-life in the religion of ancient Egypt to the Zulu view of the afterlife.

Tips for Answering

Some essay questions will ask you to compare two ideas or things; some essay questions will ask you to compare and contrast. You may find that some of your professors draw a distinction between the tasks of "comparing" and of "contrasting". For some people, to compare is to find similarities, and to contrast is to find divergences. Some of the essay questions in this book should be read in this way. The above essay question, however, is using the word "compare" in a different manner. Here "to compare" means to examine two (in this case) concepts in order to discover how they are alike _and_ how they are different. A comparison between Japanese and American management styles would not just tell you how they are alike, but would also point up where they differ. The essay assignment, therefore, is to draw out for your readers both the differences and the similarities in how these two cultures viewed the problem of immortality.

An interesting and insightful comparison between two things or ideas will probably not be a simple comparison. For example, if you are comparing Japanese and American management you might find that in some respects they are the same, but in other respects they are different. You would be analyzing the larger question into smaller questions, or points (in this case, "management structure", "decision-making process", "group dynamics", etc.). To prepare for a comparison of the Egyptian and Mesopotamian views of immortality, you might want to list the points for comparison. Such points, for instance, could include each religion's view of the gods, of the human soul, of the nature of human existence, and of the after-life. There are certainly others you might want to list. In listing each point you might discover that the two religions are quite close in how they see some points, and quite different in how they view others.

Once you have broken down the larger issue, you need to decide how you are going to integrate these individual points into a unified essay. In general, there are two ways to structure a comparison essay: by <u>block</u> or by <u>point</u>. To compare by block, in this case, would mean to discuss first, point by point, the Egyptian view of immortality. Then, after concluding an analysis of the Egyptian view, you would discuss, point by point, the Zulu view. It would be important, of course, when you are discussing the material from Zulu religion to refer back and contrast this view to the Egyptian view discussed earlier. To compare by point, on the other hand, would mean to discuss first the Egyptian view of the gods, and then the Zulu deities. Subsequently, you would discuss in tandem their views of the soul, and so on. This method means alternating constantly from one religion to the other. Both methods have their strengths and weaknesses; which is best for you to use will depend on your writing style and your arguments. In both cases, however, you would want to end your essay by summarizing your conclusions and discussing the implications of these conclusions for our view of these two cultures.

PART NINE PROJECTS FOR DEVELOPING RELIGIOUS EMPATHY

1. The Kingdoms of Egypt described in this chapter of the textbook have ceased to exist. The art and the culture

that they produced, however, still exists and continues to excite our imaginations. Art from Egypt has been installed in museums throughout Europe and America. This preservation has not been without controversy; some Egyptians believe that their art was plundered from their country and should be returned to them. Whatever position one takes on this issue, it does seem clear that the museums have had some role in preserving and restoring much of this art. It is through the art of Egypt that many of us can most directly enter into the world of the Pharaohs.

If you are in a city fortunate enough to have a collection of Egyptian art, take an afternoon to visit and view the collection. (If you do not have access to a collection of Egyptian art, you might want to examine pictures of Egyptian art in a history of world art in your library. Just bear in mind that a picture is only a faint reflection of the original.) Take your time to stroll the gallery, examine the objects and read the explanations concerning each object. Is some of the art familiar to you? Are any of the statues or paintings representations of gods or rulers discussed in this chapter? What seems to be the way in which humans are portrayed in the art? Is there a difference in the way men and women are portrayed? If the collection is comprehensive, notice the way in which man is portrayed in works of the Early Dynastic Period, the Middle Kingdom and the New Kingdom. Try to address these questions as you view the art: What are the differences, if any, in the portrayals? Are the works of some periods more rigid and formal, and those of other periods more soft and informal? Would some of the works be seen as more geometric and some be seen as more realistic? What does this art tell us about the changes impinging on Egyptian society and culture during these three periods? What does it show us about Egyptian religion?

2. A project involving African art requires some drawing. When you are in a museum with a collection of African art, see if you can find an object that interests you and is identified as from the Yoruba people. (This project would work with art from any other African society.) The works that you find might be in the form of a mask, or it might be a cult figurine or a door. Art and spirituality have always been intimately connected in African art. A mask as used by the Yoruba during the Gelede festival illustrates this point, since it is not designed to be

merely viewed as a stationary object. Rather it can also be used and experienced in a religious ritual involving music and dance to celebrate seasonal changes and to honor the powerful women in the society.

After you have selected an object, do the following: First, make a careful sketch of the object. When you are drawing the object, try to be aware of the proportions of the objects and how it is constructed. Also, try to envision how it might be used in a ritual itself. If you have done additional reading on the Yoruba, imagine how theater, dance, art and music might all be combined in the mask and its use. Second, go to the library and do some research on the art and religion of the Yoruba. Try to find pictures of similar objects, and study how they are used in Yoruba culture and religion. Third, write down a brief response in your sketch book, commenting on how the object illuminates the culture that produced it. If you find this helpful, you might get in the habit of keeping a combination sketch-note book for museum trips. Drawing an object often makes us more aware of the structure of the object, the technique of the artist, and its use in society and religion.

3. Every culture has a slightly different view of death and the status of ancestors. As you read in Chapter Two of the textbook, the role of ancestors is very important in many forms of African religion.

   You might remember an aunt or uncle, or some even more distant relative, who has passed away. This would be an ancestor of yours. Think about, if you wish, what role this person now plays in your life. What would it mean to say that this ancestor still has some connection to your life? How would you describe this role ("I remember her." "I feel his presence." etc.)? After you have thought about how ancestors connect, or do not connect, to your life, compare that view to the roles of ancestors in traditional African religion. How are they different? How are they the same? In that they are different is the difference due to your identifying with a different religious tradition? Is it due to the difference between a traditional society and a modern, technological society? Is there anything we might be able to learn from the African view of ancestors?

ANSWER KEY TO SELF-TEST SECTION

B) Multiple Choice

1. a	6. b
2. c	7. a
3. d	8. b
4. c	9. a
5. d	10. b

C) True-False

1. T	6. T
2. F	7. T
3. T	8. T
4. F	9. F
5. F	10. T

Notes

[1]"Hymn to the god Aton," J. H. Breasted, The Dawn of Consciousness (New York: Charles Scribner's Sons, 1934) 284-286.

PART TWO
Religions Arising in India

PART ONE LEARNING OBJECTIVES

Doing these exercises, in conjunction with reading the textbook, should help you to achieve the following objectives. Read them and see how many you already have mastered; then study the following terms and concepts, and work through the exercises. After you have completed all the exercises, return to this section and review the objectives again.

You should be able to:

1. Identify the four major religions that have originated in India, and explain briefly when and how each tradition began.

2. Name at least three characteristics that most of these four traditions share.

PART TWO TERMS AND INDIVIDUALS

A) Terms and Concepts

Hinduism

Jainism

Buddhism
soul
reincarnation
Sikhism
rebirth
karma

B) Individuals

Parshva
Siddhartha Gautama
Nanak
Mahavira
Buddha

C) Individuals and Terms From Other Traditions

Islam
the Prophet Muhammad

PART THREE GUIDED REVIEW

1. Four major religious traditions have arisen in India. These four are: ______________, ________________, ________________, and _________________.

2. Scholars are not always able to understand all aspects concerning how these religions began, in part due to the fact that ____________________________.

3. Hinduism began about ____________________.

4. The founder of Jainism was ________________.

5. Buddhism was founded in the ___________ century ______, by ___________.

6. Sikhism was founded in the ___________ century _______, and it can be traced back to a revelation received by _______________.

7. Sikhism can be said to incorporate elements of both ________________, and _________________.

8. Three characteristics that are shared by these four traditions (with some exceptions for Buddhism) are ____________________________, ____________________________, and ___________________________.

PART FOUR QUESTIONS FOR CONSIDERATION

As you study the religions of India and read Part II of the textbook try to reflect upon, and even write out, responses to the following questions. These questions are designed to help you synthesize what you are learning about Indian religions, and reach your own conclusions concerning the significance of these traditions.

1. The textbook claims that the religions of India should be considered a "family of religions" because they share certain characteristics. What are these characteristics? Can you identify any other shared characteristics besides the ones mentioned in the book?

2. Buddhism does not share a number of these characteristics. How would you explain the relation of Buddhism to the other religions of India? What central elements does it share with religions such as Hinduism and Jainism?

3. After you have studied the religions of China and Japan, and those of the Family of Abraham, try to compare the central characteristics of Indian religion to those of these two other families of religions.

Chapter 3
Hinduism

PART ONE LEARNING OBJECTIVES

Doing these exercises, in conjunction with reading the textbook, should help you to achieve the following objectives. Read them and see how many you already have mastered; then study the following terms and concepts, and work through the exercises. After you have completed all the exercises, return to this section and review the objectives again.

You should be able to:

1. Discuss the pre-Aryan Dravidian civilization, what is known about this culture and its religious practices, the Aryan invasion, and the resulting synthesis of the Aryan and Dravidian religious traditions.

2. Name the main groups of Hindu scriptures that were produced during the Vedic, Epic and later periods, describe their nature and relations to each other, and understand the difference between "shruti" and "smriti".

3. Describe the nature and characteristics of Vedic religion, including a discussion of the major Vedic deities, how they are portrayed in The Veda and the nature of Vedic worship.

4. Analyze the development of Hinduism from Vedic religion to the Upanishads, including a discussion of the development of different beliefs and practices during these periods.

5. Discuss the doctrine of Brahman-Atman as it is presented in the Upanishads, and, in particular, what this doctrine says about the nature of man, and man's relation to the Universe and the Absolute.

6. Describe the system of social stratification known as "varna", and how the ideas of "karma" and "samsara" are used in Hinduism to justify this system.

7. Explain the central problem that Arjuna faces in the <u>Bhagavad Gita</u>, and delineate and illustrate each of the four ways to moksha.

8. Describe the Four Goals of Life, the Four Stages of Life and the Four Ways to Salvation, and explain how each might function in the life of a Hindu.

9. Name the six schools of Hindu philosophy, and give a brief description of the basic positions of each school.

10. Refer to specific texts from the Hindu scriptures in order to analyze and illustrate the fundamental characteristics of Vedic religion, Brahmanism, Upanishadic Hinduism and the approach of the <u>Bhagavad Gita</u>.

11. Show how Hinduism has developed since the ninth century C.E. in reaction to new influences and new challenges (in particular, how Hinduism has reacted to influences from the West), and recognize the major Hindu thinkers from this period.

12. Discuss the changing role of women in modern India and Hinduism, and give examples of women and feminine aspects of the Absolute that have played significant roles in Hinduism.

13. Discuss and write about the Hindu Worldview; in particular, the Hindu view of The Absolute, the universe, the human role in the universe, the fundamental problem and resolution for human beings, community and ethics, history, rituals and symbols, and other religious traditions.

14. Define the concept of karma, analyze how this concept was expressed and refined in the Veda and the Upanishads, and

discuss how the Law of Karma is related to the ideas of samsara and caste.

PART TWO TERMS AND INDIVIDUALS

A) Terms and Concepts

Hinduism	Indus Valley (Civilization)
Dravidian people	Aryan people
devas	asuras
varna	caste
shruti	smriti
Purusha	Agni
Indra	soma
Varuna	Rita
Brihaspati	Mitra
Brahmin	darshana
Yama	rishis
Brahman	atman
maya	guru
tat tvam asi	monism
dualism	prakriti
moksha	saguna Brahman
nirguna Brahman	kalpa
reincarnation	(Law of) Karma
samsara	Shudras
Vaishyas	Kshatriyas
Krishna	jnana yoga
raja yoga	bhakti yoga
kama	artha
dharma	samadhi
four stages of life	
sannyasin	karma yoga
avidya	Brahma
Vishnu	Shiva
Parvati	Kali
Durga	Ganesh
avatar	Lakshmi
Rama	Sita
Shaivism	Vaishnavism
Sankhya philosophy	purusha
Advaita Vedanta	Yoga
Nyaya	Vaisheshika
Purva-Mimamsa	Brahmo Samaj
Arya Samaj	jatis
untouchables	Harijans

satyagraha
ahimsa
sat-chit-ananda
Nataraja
henotheism
samskaras
upanayana
janeu
vivaha
antyesti
shraddha
puja
Theosophy
kirtana
International Society for Krishna Consciousness (ISKCON)

B) Individuals

Yajnavalkya
Uddalaka
Maitreyi
Gargi Vacaknavi
Svetaketu
Kapila
Patanjali
Shankara
Gautama
Kanada
Jaimini
Arjuna
Ram Mohan Roy
Debendranath Tagore
Ramakrishna
Dayananda Sarasvati
Swami Vivekananda
Rabindranath Tagore
Mohandas K. Gandhi
Sri Aurobindo
Sarvepalli Radhakrishnan
Indira Gandhi
Ma Jnanananda
Madame Blavatsky
Abhay Charyan De

C) Texts

Veda
Rig-Veda
Yajur-Veda
Sama-Veda
Artharva-Veda
Brahmanas
Aranyakas
Upanishads
Vedanta
Agamas
Laws of Manu
Itihasa-Purana
Mahabharata
Ramayana
Purusha sukta
samhitas
Bhagavad Gita
Puranas
Tantras
Yoga Sutra

D) Individuals and Terms From Other Traditions

Haoma
Tirthankaras
Jains
Mahavira
Siddhartha Gautama
Buddhism
Islam
Allah
Kabir
Nanak
Sikhism
Christianity
St. Thomas
moira
Plato
Immanuel Kant
Nanak
Kabir

Socrates
Pythagoras

PART THREE GUIDED REVIEW

1. The earliest Indian civilization for which we have evidence is that of ______________. Based on archaeological evidence, this civilization could be described as ____.

2. Beginning around 1000 B.C.E. a large group of nomadic people began to migrate into India. These people were called the _______________, which means ______________.

3. These invaders honored their gods by ___________________.

4. According to some scholars this conquest of one people by another may have been the origin of the system of social stratification known as _______________. This predated the more rigid system of social stratification that is usually known as the ______________________.

5. Hindu scriptures can be classified into two categories: _______________, which means _____________ and _______________, which means ______________.

6. Revealed writings are known in Hinduism as ________. The earliest Hindu scriptures are collections of text called the ___________.

7. The most important of the four collections that make up the oldest part of shruti is known as the ________________. It could be described as _________________________________

8. The hymns of the Veda are addressed to a great variety of gods. However, among the more important gods were:
   a. ______________, the warrior god who slays demons.
   b. ______________, the sky god and the protector of moral order/truth.
   c. ______________, the moral order and truth which underlies the Universe.
   d. ______________, the god who personifies an agreement or contract.
   e. ______________, the god of fire and the sacrifice.

9. Brahmins, when they were performing the sacrifice, dug __________ pits which were used to _________________.

10. The group of texts called the Brahmanas were _____________________________ on the Veda. The Brahmanas represent a change from the Veda in that they ____.

11. The thinkers whose insights are recorded in the Upanishads are termed ______________. Many scholars believe that these thinkers came from castes rebelling against ___________________________________.

12. The texts called the Upanishads were written down in the time period from ____________ to ______________.

13. Central to many of the Upanishads is the search for a unity or permanence in the midst of the changing totality of things. For many of the Upanishadic thinkers the permanence they found was called the ______________ or _______________.

14. The Absolute Reality which is the ground of all things and which transcends all things is called in many of the Upanishads _____________. The subjective force which is equated with this Reality is called _________________. These two are perceived as being different due to _______.

15. For Hinduism, Brahman can be viewed in two ways: either as _________________________, the personal Absolute with attributes, or as _______________________, the impersonal Absolute which transcends all attributes.

16. The process of cycles of reincarnation that could stretch over many lives is called _____________. This process is governed by the moral law of action and reaction which is called the law of _______________.

17. The four major groups within the caste system are _______________, _______________, _______________ and _______________. A fifth group who were literally "outside the caste system" were ____________.

18. In the Bhagavad Gita Krishna explains to Arjuna that there are four ways to obtain release: the way of __________, the way of _______________, the way of ________________, and the way of _______________.

19. Hinduism allows it adherents to choose from among four different goals of life: ________________, ________________, ________________ and ________________.

20. Hinduism believes that there are four stages in the life of an upper-caste male Hindu; these four stages are ________________, ________________, ________________ and ________________. Women observe three stages, not be expected to become a ________________.

21. According to karma yoga, the most important duty for a Hindu male householder is ________________. On the other hand, among important duties for women would be ________________.

22. Literally thousands of deities are worshipped by contemporary Hindus, but three deities are the most popular: ________________, ________________ and ________________.

23. The god Krishna is held to be an avatar of ____________.

24. The book that contains the precepts and moral codes which all Hindus are expected to follow is ________________.

25. The Samkya school was a dualistic school of philosophy that believed there were two realities in the universe, ________________ and ________________.

26. The greatest thinker of the Advaita Vedanta school was ______________. He argued that the world of appearance is ____________, while the one true Reality is ______________.

27. The other four schools of Hindu philosophy are ________________, ________________, ________________ and ________________.

28. The Hindu reformer Ram Mohan Roy, in rejecting established Hindu beliefs such as polytheism, and in rejecting Hindu customs such as infanticide of females, was influenced by ______________________________.

29. The important modern Hindu leader who preached the power of love, and fought for social justice and Indian independence was ______________________________.

30. Women in modern India have been able to assume leadership roles that would have been unthinkable in traditional India. A woman who dominated the politics and government in India was ________________, and a woman who has assumed an

exceptional religious role is ____________________.

31. The problem that the Aryans had in describing the forces of the universe was ________________________. Many Hindu leaders addressed this problem by holding that it was better to ______________________ than to ______________________.

32. While the labels of "polytheism" or "monotheism" may not be appropriate for Hinduism, a more appropriate term may be ________________. Perhaps a distinctive attitude of Hinduism towards the Absolute is the belief that behind all phenomenon lies ____________________________.

33. Many more Hindus prefer to worship deities such as Kali or Krishna, rather than deities such as Brahma, because they are more ___________________________.

34. Hinduism rejects the view that humans are made up of only their physical bodies; for Hinduism the body is but a covering for __________________________.

35. The human problem for Hinduism is __________________.

36. For Hinduism the solution for humans is ________________ _________________________________. For many Hindus this requires assistance from _____________________.

37. While Hindus have great respect for all animals, it is of special merit to express compassion for one particular animal: the ________________.

38. The Hindu view of history is a ___________________ view.

39. Samskaras can be defined as __________________________.

40. Among the most important rites of Hindus are: the upanayana sacrament ______________________, the vivaha rite ____________________, and the shraddha ____________________.

41. Recently, relations in India between Hindus, Muslims and Sikhs have been ______________________________________.

42. Two religious traditions that have been inspired by Hinduism and that have gained followers in the West are ________________ and __________________.

43. In the Bhagavad Gita the Lord Krishna assures the young warrior Arjuna that he can neither ________________ or _____________________.

44. The cycle or succession of states of existence that an individual goes through is termed ____________________.

45. The basic meaning of the term "karma" is ______________. The solution to the Law of Karma is ________________________.

PART FOUR ANALYZING TEXTS

Below are three texts that were not in the textbook. The texts, however, do contain ideas and concepts with which you should be familiar after reading the textbook and studying the selections in the textbook from primary religious documents. Read each text carefully, compare it to the primary documents you have studied and try to analyze each by answering the following questions: What are the main ideas in the text? What viewpoint or viewpoints might the author of the text represent? Is it possible to identify the specific thinker, discipline, movement, tradition or work from which the text derives? What intellectual, literary, social, cultural or historical influences are reflected in the text? For each of your conclusions, try to point to specific evidence in the text (e.g. terms, ideas, arguments, writing style, etc.) which supports your conclusion. Be careful that your conclusions do not exceed the evidence upon which they rest.

TEXT ONE

Higher than this is Brahman. The Supreme, the Great
Hidden in all things, body by body,
The One embracer of the universe-
By knowing Him as Lord men become immortal.

I know this mighty person
Of the colour of the sun, beyond darkness.
Only by knowing Him does one pass over death.
There is no other path for going there.

Than whom there is naught else higher,
Than whom there is naught smaller, naught greater,
The One stand like a tree established in heaven.
By Him, the Person, this whole world is filled. [1]

TEXT TWO

Those who fixing their minds on Me worship Me, ever earnest and possessed of supreme faith - them do I consider most perfect in yoga.

But those who worship the Imperishable, the Undefinable, the Unmanifested, the Omnipresent, the Unthinkable, the Unchanging and the Immobile, the Constant,

By restraining all the senses, being even-minded in all conditions, rejoicing in the welfare of all creatures - they come to Me indeed [just like the others].

The difficulty of those whose thoughts are set on the Unmanifested is greater, for the goal of the Unmanifested is hard to reach by embodied beings.[2]

TEXT THREE

What sin we have committed against an intimate, O Varuna, against a friend or companion at any time, a brother, a neighbor, or a stranger, that, O Varuna, loose from us.

If like gamblers at play we have cheated, whether in truth or without knowing, all that loose from us, O God. So may we be dear to thee, O Varuna. [3]

PART FIVE SELF-TEST

A) Definitions and Descriptions - Write your own definition or description of each of the following terms, individuals or texts. After completing the self-test, check your answer with the definition or description given in the textbook.

1. dharma ____
____
____.

2. Indra ____
____
____.

3. Laws of Manu ____
____
____.

4. nirguna Brahman ____
____
____.

5. Ram Mohan Roy ____
____
____.

6. karma yoga ____
____
____.

7. Brahmins ____
____
____.

8. Veda ____
____
____.

9. Shankara ____
____
____.

10. Atman ____
____
____.

B) Multiple Choice

1. According to many of the Upanishads the Ultimate Reality is

   a. Prakriti
   b. Maya
   c. Brahman
   d. Brahma

2. The term in Hinduism for the organization of society on the basis of color, which predated the more rigid stratification of later periods, is

   a. Varna
   b. Veda
   c. Varuna
   d. Caste

3. The god of fire, which was very important for the Vedic sacrifice, is named

   a. Agni
   b. Indra
   c. Brahma
   d. Rita

4. Which of the following is <u>not</u> included among the list of the four goals in life?

   a. Kama - pleasure.
   b. Artha - material success.
   c. Bhakti - devotion.
   d. Dharma - duty to ones caste.

5. The rite in Hinduism which initiates a boy as a twice-born person is known as which sacrament?

   a. The upanayana.
   b. The shraddha.
   c. The samsara.
   d. The vivaha.

6. Which of the following statements is probably <u>not</u> a true statement about the Aryan people?

   a. The name Aryan means "noble people".
   b. The Aryans had a highly advanced urban civilization.
   c. The Aryans honored their gods by sacrificing animals.
   d. Many Aryan practices are reflected in the Veda.

7. The lowest group within the caste system, unable to even hear the Veda being read, was the

   a. Vaishyas
   b. Brahmins
   c. Shudras
   d. Kshatriyas

8. Which of the following best describes the gurus of the Upanishads?

 a. They were priests who officiated at sacrifices.
 b. They were thinkers who taught about the highest reality and supervised training.
 c. They were fortune tellers.
 d. They were founders of the six Hindu philosophical schools.

9. The Hindu philosophical system attributed to Kapila, which argues that the universe is made up of two radically different types of reality is

 a. Advaita Vedanta
 b. Nyaya
 c. Purva-Mimamsa
 d. Samkhya

10. The famous nineteenth century Hindu mystic who had an absolute devotion to the goddess Kali, but saw Allah, Jesus, Krishna and all deities as manifestations of one God was

 a. Ramakrishna
 b. Sri Aurobindo
 c. Radhakrishnan
 d. Rabindranath Tagore

C) True-False

T F 1. Hinduism, like Judaism and Islam, rejects the use of images in worship.

T F 2. Those Hindu writings which are seen as the direct revealed word are termed "smriti".

T F 3. One of the earliest Indian civilizations was that of the Dravidians, who lived in large cities with underground plumbing.

T F 4. Two doctrines that were at the center of Gandhi's thought were those of satyagraha and ahimsa.

T F 5. While the Upanishads have as their goal the uniting of the atman with the Brahman, not all of the Upanishads preach an absolute monism.

T F 6. Many scholars believe that the Brahmanas and the Upanishads grew out of the same movement, since both de-emphasis the role of the sacrifice.

T F 7. The movement called Arya Samaj, founded by Dayananda Sarisvati, was important in the history of modern Hinduism because it tried to embrace many elements from Christianity and the West.

T F 8. Since Indian independence, women have been able to take on new roles in Indian society, including becoming religious and secular leaders.

T F 9. In the _Bhagavad Gita_ Krishna urges Arjuna to not lay down his arms, but to enter the battle and fight as a warrior.

T F 10. According to the Advaita Vedanta school of Shankara, the world is made up of many particular things, ultimately understandable as atoms.

PART SIX ESSAY AND DISCUSSION QUESTIONS

1. Hinduism offers its believers a choice of four goals in life. Two of these goals are the pursuit of pleasure, and the pursuit of commercial or political success, goals not often associated with a religious life. What might be some advantages of offering people a choice among goals in their life? What might be some of the drawbacks?

2. What evidence does Hinduism offer in favor of the existence of the atman? Do you find the evidence convincing? What might be the most serious challenges to this theory of the atman?

3. Compare and contrast the views of the Absolute contained in the hymns to Varuna and Agni from the _Rig Veda_, and in the quote from the _Chandogya Upanishad_.

4. How would you characterize Hindu responses to the Western influence since the early 1800's? What responses appear to have best meet the challenges of Western influence, and why? Back up your analysis by using examples of specific Hindu thinkers and movements.

5. Given the wide range of practices and beliefs included in what is commonly termed "Hinduism", do you think using the term "Hinduism" to refer to such a variety of practices is helpful or unhelpful? If you think the term should be used, what criteria determines whether a belief or practice is "Hindu"? If you argue that the term is misleading, what terminology would you employ and why?

PART SEVEN CONFRONTING QUESTIONS AND ISSUES

One of the issues confronting contemporary Hinduism, as indeed it confronts all religious traditions in the modern world, is how Hindus will adjust their views on the changing roles for women in both secular and religious life. Women are becoming college educated, are following business careers and are demanding a role in choosing their own husbands. Yet the overall status of women in traditional Hindu society was, and in many ways still is, very low. In liberating themselves from some of the roles they were assigned in the past many Hindu women base their positions on Western ideas and thinkers. Many, however, also try to ground their positions in their own heritage; that is to say, the practices and ideas of Hinduism itself.

Imagine that you are a Hindu woman who wants to fashion a role for herself as a woman, a role other than that prescribed by <u>The Laws of Manu</u>. To what textual tradition, school of thought or thinker within the traditions of Hinduism might you turn to find the basis for a more equal role for women? What specific ideas or viewpoints in that tradition offers the basis for a new status for Hindu women? What might be new roles for women? You might want to do some research on a specific women religious leader, such as Swami Jnanananda, or on women's roles in such Hindu rites as puja or bhajan (devotional singing).

PART EIGHT AN ESSAY FOR DEEPER CONSIDERATION

<u>Essay Question</u>

Analyze the understand of "moksha" (liberation from re-birth and re-death) as it is revealed in the quotations from the <u>Bhagavad Gita</u> in the textbook. What is the view of the relation between soul and body underlying this quote? What evidence could be given in support of these views of the soul and body, and of the law of karma? What evidence could be given against these views? What type of possibilities exist for obtaining this release?

<u>Tips For Answering</u>

The term "analyze" can be used in various ways. In general, however, to analyze means to break something down into smaller parts in order to better understand the whole. An analysis of the question of whether capital punishment is just may reveal that three or four different questions are involved. For example, you might find that the larger issue can not be addressed before you become clear on your definition of "justice." This would appear to indicate that you are being asked to break down the larger question of the meaning of moksha as revealed in the quotations into smaller, more specific questions.

This question can be broken down into three somewhat smaller questions: 1)What is the view of "moksha" in this quotation? 2)What is the view of the soul and the body in this quotation, and how does this view serve as a basis for the view of liberation? 3)What evidence can be given in support of such views? It might be helpful to attack each part of the question separately when you are researching and writing your first drafts. While the third part of the questions almost definitely needs to be answered last, you might want to address either the first or the second part of the question in the first part of your essay. That is to say, you might first examine the relation between the soul and the body, and demonstrate how this view leads, or supports, a theory of liberation. Or, you might first look at the belief in moksha, define this term as it is used in Hinduism, and then examine how it relates to a particular view of the soul and the body.

In answering this essay question make sure that you define for your readers how you, at each moment in your essay, are defining the significant terms. For example, terms such as "reincarnation", "soul" and "body" need to be defined. How is the <u>Bhagavad Gita</u> defining these terms? Is this a definition you are using yourself?

PART NINE PROJECTS FOR DEVELOPING RELIGIOUS EMPATHY

1. When you read the textbook and study this guide the names and terms in the ancient Indian language of Sanskrit may seem unfamiliar and strange. Yet Sanskrit and English are languages that both have a common root: a now lost language called Proto-Indo-European. Many of the Sanskrit terms you have studied are cognates with English words. For example, the Sanskrit term "Trimurti" (meaning the Vedic trinity of the gods Brahma, Vishnu and Shiva) has the same part "tri" (three) as the English word "tricycle".

   The American Heritage Dictionary of the English Language has an appendix which is a list of Indo-European roots. If you have a copy of this dictionary, or if the library has a copy, try the following: Look up the English words "video", "right" and "firm" in the dictionary. At the end of the citation for each word will be its Indo-European root. For each word look up the root in the Appendix. What Sanskrit terms that you already know are related to these common English words? How has the form of the word seemed to change over time and between languages? Can you discover any other English cognates of Sanskrit terms?

2. Many cities and universities have museums of art or anthropology which contain collections of Indian art. You may already be familiar with one in your area, either through trips for an art history class or through going on your own. If you are not sure if such resources exist near you, the reference librarian at your college or university library should be able to show you reference books that list the museums in the United States and detail their collections. Your instructor might know of any collections of Indian art near you.

   If you are fortunate enough to be near a museum with a collection of Indian art, get together with a friend and take a trip to the museum. Notice whether there are any objects from the early Dravidian civilization, perhaps clay seals, or sculptures of the human figure. What do these pieces tell you about the civilization that produced them? What do they tell you about the physical nature of the Dravidians. Next, see whether any works are identified as being of the Gupta Period. How do these works differ from the earlier works? If there are statues of any of the Hindu gods, how are they portrayed? What aspects of the Hindu view of the Absolute, of man and of the universe can you see reflected in these works? If there any more recent Indian works of art in the collection to what extent do these works reflect Hindu ideas and values? To what extent do they reflect ideas and values from other cultures?

3. In 1893 Swami Vivekânanda came to the United States to represent Hinduism at the World Parliament of Religions in Chicago. Since this time many representatives of Hinduism have journeyed to the United States to teach and to start religious communities. Vivekânanda himself organized a number of Vedantic centers in the United States. These centers, named after Vivekânanda's teacher, are part of the Ramakrishna Mission.

If you feel comfortable with the idea, you might think about arranging a visit to a Ramakrishna Mission, a yoga center or some other Hindu group in your area. You might want to first research the groups in your area, and find out some information on their beliefs and practices. You may feel more comfortable visiting with one or two classmates, rather than just by yourself. Contact the group that you are interested in visiting prior to your actual visit. Explain that you are taking a course in World Religions, and your visit would be in order to complete a class project. While you would like to understand more about Hinduism, and the teachings of this particular branch, you should also emphasize that you are not seeking to join the group, or become an adherent. If the members of the community do not feel comfortable with your stance, than you might want to suggest that you not visit.

If the community is open to having a number of you visit, observe their practices and ask questions, then try to model the role of the religious scholar. Notice what are the beliefs of the group, and what are the practices. Which of the Hindu traditions that you have studied seem to have most influenced this community? Have any of the beliefs and practices been changed for the Western audience? How so? What roles do women play in the community, and are these the same roles as those for men? What might account for these roles for men and women?

ANSWER KEY TO SELF-TEST SECTION

B) Multiple Choice

1. c	6. b
2. a	7. c
3. a	8. b
4. c	9. d
5. a	10. a

C) True-False

1. F	6. F
2. F	7. F
3. T	8. T
4. T	9. T
5. T	10. F

Notes

[1]Svetâsvatara Upanishad, III. 7-9, R. E. Hume, trans., in A Sourcebook in Indian Philosophy, ed. Sarvepalli Radhakrishnan and Charles A. Moore, (Princeton, N. J.: Princeton University Press, 1957) 90-91.

[2]The Bhagavadgîtâ, XII: 1-5, trans. Sarvepalli Radhakrishnan (New York: Harper & Row, 1973) 291-293.

[3]Rg Veda, V: 85, trans. Edward J. Thomas, in A Sourcebook in Indian Philosophy, ed. Sarvepalli Radhakrishnan and Charles A. Moore (Princeton, N. J.: Princeton University Press, 1957) 29.

Chapter 4
Buddhism

PART ONE LEARNING OBJECTIVES

Doing these exercises, in conjunction with reading the textbook, should help you to achieve many of the following objectives. Read them and see how many you already have mastered; then study the following terms and concepts, and work through the exercises. After you have completed all the exercises, review the objectives again.

You should be able to:

1. Understand how some religious belief systems have formed around a central historical figure and personality, and what issues arise when scholars attempt to interpret stories of the person's life.

2. Outline the life of Siddhartha Gautama, the Buddha, and discuss the significance for Buddhism of the central events in his life.

3. Explain the central teachings of the Buddha, and analyze the significance of his teachings. In particular, you should be able to explain the Buddhist teachings of The Four Noble Truths, pratitya-samutpada, The Middle Path, Samsara and Nirvana, and questions which do not tend to edification.

4. Name the main divisions into which Buddhist scripture is divided, and describe the nature of each group of writings and how they came to be written down.

5. Analyze the development of Buddhism in India from the death of the Buddha to the appearance of the Mahayana Schools. In particular, you should be able to talk about the role of King Ashoka, and the respective positions of the Theravda and Mahayana branches of Buddhism.

6. Give a brief description of at least two Indian Mahayana Schools, and explain how their positions differed from earlier Buddhism.

7. Show how Buddhism changed after its arrival in China, and name at least four Chinese Buddhist schools and give a brief description of their basic positions.

8. Describe the development of Buddhism in Japan, and name at least five Japanese Buddhist schools and give a brief description of their basic positions.

9. Give the main outline of the history of Buddhism in Tibet.

10. Compare and contrast the forms of Buddhism that originated and developed in India, China, Japan and Tibet, focusing particularly on how Buddhism adapted to a variety of cultures, and how the Buddhist realization was expressed in variety of forms.

11. Understand how Buddhism has had an influence in America and Europe, and what issues and challenges confront Buddhism in this new environment.

12. Discuss and write about the Buddhist Worldview; in particular, discuss and write about the Buddhist view of The Absolute, the world, the human role in the world, the fundamental problem and resolution for human beings, community and ethics, history, symbols, life after death and Buddhism's relation to other religions.

13. Define in general terms the concept of "Nirvana", discuss the "positive" and "negative" aspects of Nirvana, and illustrate how the terms was used by schools in both the Theravadin and Mahayana traditions.

PART TWO TERMS AND INDIVIDUALS

A) Terms and Concepts

Bodhgaya
Buddha
The Four Passing Sights
The Bo Tree
Mara
Sakya clan
The Middle Path (Middleway)
The Four Noble Truths
Sangha
dharma
The Ten Precepts
The Three Jewels
dukkha
tanha
The Eightfold Path
jhana
skandhas
no-Self (anatta)
samsara
karma
Nirvana
Tathagata
sutra (sutta)
Theravada
Mahayana
Sthaviras
Mahasamghikas
arhat
Maitreya Buddha
Hinayana
Bodhisattva
Avalokitishvara (Guanyin)
Madhyamika School
pratitya-samutpada
avidya
Yogacara School
Tian Tai School (Tendai)
Hua-Yen School
Vairocana Buddha (Dainichi)
Suchness
Chan School (Zen)
Pure Land School (Jingtu/Jôdo)
Amitabha Buddha (Amida)
Three Kingdoms Period
Shingon Sect (Chen Yen)
Rhôbu Shintô
mantra
mudras
mandala
"Namu Amida Butsu"
Hôzô Bosatsu
Jôdô Shinshû Sect
Dhyana
Lin Chi Sect (Rinzai)
Ts'ao-tung Sect (Sôtô)
satori
koan (kung-an)
Nichiren Sect
"Namu Myôhô-renge-kyô"
tantric Buddhism
Tara
Kalachakra
puja
Nyingmapa
Gelugpa
lama
The Dalai Lama
Soka Gakkai
Kômeito party
Buddhist Churches of America
Buddhist Virha Society
Nyingmapa Meditation Center
Karme-Choling
Trikaya
Nirmanakaya
Dharmakaya
Sambhogakaya
compassion (karuna)
wisdom (prajña)

B) Individuals

Queen Maya	Siddhartha Gautama (Sakyamuni)
King Suddhodana	Yasodhara
Rahula	Alara Kalama
Uddaka Ramaputta	Sujata
Sariputra	Uruvela Kashyapa
Ananda	Mahakashyapa
Devadatta	Mahajapati
Nagasena	King Milinda (King Menander)
Malunkyaputta	Kisogotami
King Mahapadma	King Ashoka
King Kanishka	Chandragupta
Nagarjuna	Asanga
Mahendra	Sanghamitta
Mou Tzu	Zhiyi
Fa Zang	Bodhidharma
Emperor T'aejong	Emperor Kimmei
Soga clan	Empress Suiko
Shôtoku Taishi	Saichô (Dyengo Daishi)
Kukai (Kôbô Daishi)	Ryônin
Hônen Shônin (Genku)	Shinran
Nichiren	Padma-Sambhava
U Nu	Thich Tri Quang
Thich Thien Minh	Makiguchi Tsunesaburo
D. T. Suzuki	Soryu Kaghi
Soven Shaku	Daisaku Ikeda
Tsultrim Allione (J.Ewing)	Jiyu Kennett Roshi

C) Texts

Kanjur	Tanjur
Tripitaka	Vinaya Pitaka
Sutta Pitaka	Abhidhamma Pitaka
Mahavibhasa	jatakas
The Chronicles of Ceylon	The Disputation of Error
Avatamsaka Sutra	Lotus Sutra/Saddharma-Pundarika
The Heart Sutra	Red Annals
Anguttara-nikâya	Samyutta-nikâya
Pañcavimsatisâhasrikâ	Sukhâvativyûha

D) Individuals and Terms From Other Traditions

Brahmanism	Hinduism
Brahmin	Kshatriyas
brahmacharya	Alexander The Great
Jainism	Neo-Confucianism
Mao Tse-tung	mu
mudang	Shinto

Amaterasu
Hatha Yoga
Karl Marx
Thomas Merton
Bon
Shakti cults
Marxism

PART THREE GUIDED REVIEW

1. Brahmanism and Buddhism differed in their description of the problem for humans. Brahmanism saw the problem as ______________________________. Buddhism, however, saw the problem as ____.

2. One difference between Hinduism and Buddhism is that Buddhism begins with ______________________________.

3. The name of the person who would become the Buddha was ________________________, and he was later known as ________________________.

4. The four sights that Siddhartha saw were ________________, ______________________, ________________________, and ______________________.

5. After Siddhartha decided that he could not find what he sought from his teachers he embarked on a course of ________ ____. At the last moment he realized that this path was ______________________.

6. The Four Noble Truths that the Buddha first taught in the Deer Park at Sarnath were the Noble Truth concerning ______________, concerning ______________________, concerning ____, and concerning ____.

7. When one is initiated into Buddhism, one takes a vow to take refuge in the ________________, the ________________, and the _______________________.

8. Ordinary human existence is dukkha, which the Buddhists take to mean ____ ____.

9. The Buddhists, unlike most of the Hindu schools, did not believe man had a ________________. Instead, they believed that man was comprised of the Five _________________.

10. Both the Hindus and the Buddhists believed that life was a cycle of rebirths, termed ________________. This cycle was governed by the power of _________________.

11. When this cycle of death and rebirth is brought to an end, the Buddhists term this _____________, which means literally ___________________.

12. The collected Buddhist scripture is gathered together in the __________________________, which means ____________ _________________. These are the ___________________, the __________________________, and the _______________.

13. The two major branches of Buddhism are the ____________, and the __________________.

14. A being who delays his own entry into Nirvana in order to help all sentient beings attain Nirvana is termed a __________________________. The type of Buddhism that would use this term in this manner is _________________ Buddhism.

15. The Madhyamika School, usually associated with the philosopher ____________________, taught that _______________ ____.

16. The Yogacara School, whose greatest thinker was _________________ taught that ______________________________ ____.

17. Buddhism began in China around the year ______________.

18. Pure Land Buddhism believed that a person should look to ______________________ for help, and should say the name ______________________________________.

19. The monk who brought Chan Buddhism to China from India was ________________________. The world "Chan" itself means _______________________________.

20. The native religion of Korea was called ____________, and that of Tibet was termed _____________.

21. Buddhism was important in Japan, in part, because the importation of Buddhism also resulted in the arrival in Japan of ___________________________.

22. Saichô was the founder in Japan of the _______________ sect, while Kukai founded the ________________ sect.

23. Kukai believed that at the absolute level joining the real world of ideas with it phenomenal counterpart is ________________ Buddha, also known as _________________.

24. Three means that Shingon uses to express the Absolute are _______________, ________________, and ________________.

25. Hônen did not believe that one could reach salvation through ones own efforts, but instead had to rely upon ____________________________.

26. Shinran broke with Buddhist tradition in that he ________ _______________ and he _____________________________.

27. Shinran viewed human nature as ________________________ ____.

28. The Sanskrit word for "meditation", dhyana, came to be used for the name of a sect of Buddhism: _________ in Chinese, and _________ in Japanese.

29. The two major branches of Zen Buddhism were the ______________ branch, which emphasized _________________ ______________________________________, and the ___________ _____________ branch, which emphasized ____________________ ____.

30. The Zen Buddhist practice which takes its name from the Chinese word for "case study" is known today in Japanese as ______________.

31. Two examples of art forms that have been influenced by Zen Buddhism are _________________ and __________________.

32. The Japanese Buddhist prophet who emphasized reliance only on the Lotus Sutra was __________________.

33. The native religion of Tibet is _______________.

34. The form of Buddhism common in Tibet is called ____________________ Buddhism.

35. Three practices that are stressed in Tibetan Buddhism are:

a) mantras, which are ________________________________.
b) mandalas, which are _______________________________.
c) mudras, which are ________________________________.

36. The two major branches of Tibetan Buddhism are the ______________________, who wear __________ hats, and the ______________________, who wear __________ hats.

37. The Gelugpa sect finds replacements for the head of their orders through ____________________________________.

38. The Buddhist politician who combined Buddhism and socialism in Burma was __________________________.

39. The Buddhist left-wing political party in Japan is the _____________________________.

40. The famous Japanese teacher of Zen Buddhism who did much to popularize Zen in the West was _______________________.

41. Two Western women who have achieved leadership roles in Buddhism are ___________________ and _____________________.

41. The Buddhist doctrine that all things are impermanent is called in Pali ______________ .

42. While it might not be correct to say Buddha did not believe in gods, it is probably correct to say that he viewed them as ____.

43. For Buddhism, the central human problem is that of ________________, and the central message of Buddhism is how to ________________________________.

44. The central Buddhist social virtue is ______________, which is usually translated as compassion for all sentient beings.

45. While Buddhism did not believe in the Atman, it did believe in _____________________________________.

46. For Theravada Buddhism, Nivrana can be understood in both a positive and negative aspect:

a) ____.
b) ____.

PART FOUR ANALYZING TEXTS

Below are three texts that were not in the textbook. The texts, however, do contain ideas and concepts with which you should be familiar after reading the textbook and studying the selections in the textbook from primary religious documents. Read each text carefully, compare it to the primary documents you have studied, and try to analyze each by answering the following questions: What are the main ideas in the text? What viewpoint or viewpoints might the author of the text represent? Is it possible to identify the specific thinker, discipline, movement, tradition or work from which the text derives? What intellectual, literary, social, cultural or historical influences are reflected in the text? For each of your conclusions, try to point to specific evidence in the text (e.g. terms, ideas, arguments, writing style, etc.) which supports your conclusion. Be careful that your conclusions do not exceed the evidence upon which they rest.

TEXT ONE

Subhuti: How is perfect wisdom marked?

The Lord: It is marked with the non-attachment of space. It is, however, no mark, nor does it have one.

Subhuti: Would it be possible for all dharmas to be found by the same mark by which the perfection of wisdom is to be found?

The Lord: So it is, Subhuti, so it is. The mark by which perfect wisdom exists, through just that mark all dharmas also exist. Because all dharmas are isolated in their own-being, empty in their own-being. In that way all dharmas exist through the mark by which perfect wisdom exists, i.e. through the mark of emptiness. . . [1]

TEXT TWO

"Already, when a person has faith that he will be saved by the power of the Original Vow of Amida Buddha, and that it is possible for him to be born in the Pure Land, and already, when by believing this, there arises in him the heart of Faith which is the foundation for the mental activity such as calling-out to and reciting the Name of Amida Buddha (Nembutsu), already previous to this time Amida Buddha has conferred on us the Grace which brings us to His salvation."

"The Vow of Amida Buddha does not discriminate between the old and the young, the virtuous and the wicked. You must understand that in Amida Buddha's Vow, the essential key to receiving salvation is Faith, and only Faith. The reason for this is because Amida established His Vow precisely to try and save those people who suffer from violent cravings and intense, grave evil."

"Henceforth, for those people who have faith in the Original Vow, with the exception of invoking Amida's Name, even good actions and good works are unnecessary, since there is nothing which surpasses the excellence of the Nembutsu. I do not even fear the sins which I have committed and am committing, since there is no sin or evil which is great enough to obstruct the fulfilling of Amida Buddha's vow.[2]

TEXT THREE

Misery only doth exist, none miserable.
No doer is there; naught save the deed is found.
Nirvana is, but not the man who seeks it.
The Path exists, but not the traveler on it.[3]

PART FIVE SELF-TEST

A) Definitions and Descriptions - Write your own definition or description of each of the following terms, individuals or texts. After completing the self-test, check your answer with the definition or description given in the textbook.

1. skandhas ____
____
____.

2. Dharmakaya ____
____
____.

3. Theravada ____
____
____.

4. Nichiren sect ____
____
____.

5. Hôzô Bosatsu ____
____
____.

6. Sangha ____
____
____.

7. Buddha ____
____
____.

8. koan ____
____
____.

9. mantra ____
____
____.

10. anicca ____
____
____.

B) Multiple Choice

1. The school of Nagarjuna which taught that all dharmas are Empty (sunya) was the

   a. Sarvastavada school.
   b. Yogacara school.
   c. Madhyamika school.
   d. Theravada school.

2. The term for the Buddhist teaching of no-Self is

   a. anicca
   b. dukkha
   c. anatta
   d. ahimsa

3. Which of the following is not one of the Four Noble Truths?

   a. The truth concerning dukkha.
   b. The truth concerning the origin of dukkha.
   c. The truth concerning the cessation of dukkha.
   d. The truth concerning the continuance of dukkha.

4. The Japanese school that would make use of the <u>koan</u> is the

   a. Pure Land school.
   b. Zen school.
   c. Nichiren school.
   d. Tendai school.

5. Which of the following sights is <u>not</u> one of the Four Passing Sights that the Buddha saw?

   a. a sick man.
   b. a dead man.
   c. a poor man.
   d. an old man.

6. Which of the following is <u>not</u> one of the bodies of the Buddha mentioned in the <u>Trikaya</u> theory?

   a. Sambhogakaya
   b. Nirvanakaya
   c. Nirmanakaya
   d. Dharmakaya.

7. A Buddhist does <u>not</u> take refuge in which of these?

   a. God
   b. the Teaching
   c. the Community
   d. Buddha

8. If one was looking in the Tripitaka for the rules for monks and nuns, one would probably look in

   a. the Abhidhamma Pitaka.
   b. the Vinaya Pitaka.
   c. the Sutta Pitaka
   d. the Sangha Pitaka.

9. In what century did Buddhism probably arrive in China?

   a. first century C.E.
   b. first century B.C.E.
   c. second century C.E.
   d. second century B.C.E.

10. The Chinese sect that taught the theory of One-in-All was

a. Hua-Yen sect.
b. Chan sect.
c. Jingtu sect.
d. Tian Tai sect.

C) True-False

T F 1. The Emperor Ashoka sent many missions to various parts of Asia that spread the Buddhist teaching.

T F 2. The historical Buddha began life in India as Sakyamuni.

T F 3. The native religion of Korea is bon.

T F 4. One of the central teachings of Early Buddhism is that only the Self is permanent and unchanging.

T F 5. Shinran broke with Buddhist tradition by marrying and eating meat.

T F 6. According to tradition, Chan Buddhism was brought to China by Bodhidharma.

T F 7. The Early Buddhists differed from Hinduism in rejecting the authority of the Vedas.

T F 8. According to Theravada Buddhism, a monk who has achieved enlightenment is called a bodhisattva.

T F 9. The Tibetan Buddhist sect termed the Gelugpa are called "Red Buddhists."

T F 10. In Buddhism the goal is a state of awakening or enlightenment that is called Nirvana or Satori.

PART SIX ESSAY AND DISCUSSION QUESTIONS

1. Explain the significance that the story of the life of the Buddha would have for a Buddhist.

2. Early Buddhism attacked the belief in any kind of permanent Self or Atman. It did, however, retain a belief in reincarnation and karma. Explain how Early Buddhism could believe in reincarnation but not believe in a Self that is reincarnated.

3. Early Buddhism rejected a belief in a Soul. It also held that the notions of God and of an afterlife are, at best, irrelevant. Given these positions, should Early Buddhism be classified as a religion? Examine arguments on both sides of this question.

4. Analyze whether or not Indian Buddhism and Japanese Buddhism are so different in their worldviews and practices that they should be regarded as two different religious traditions. In your analysis consider especially the case of Pure Land Buddhism, which appears to be radically different from the teachings of the historical Buddha.

5. All schools of Buddhism claim to be a "Middleway" or "Middlepath". Compare how three schools of Buddhism - Indian Theravada Buddhism, one school of Indian Mahayana Buddhism and one school of Chinese or Japanese Buddhism - might stake out their claims to being the true Middleway.

PART SEVEN CONFRONTING QUESTIONS AND ISSUES

The textbook raises the question of how well Buddhism can adapt to the modern world and what role Buddhism can play in modern society. The answer to this question will depend, it is clear, on many factors. The attitude of the central government, and indeed the nature of the central government, in countries such as China or Cambodia will play a significant role in determining the future of Buddhism in these countries. Economic prosperity and material affluence in nations such as Japan and Taiwan will make the traditional Buddhist virtues of restraint and non-reliance on material possessions less attractive. An argument could be made, however, that one of the most pressing problems facing Buddhism today is the need to clearly articulate a relevant social philosophy. In an area of the world with pressing social problems and in which various forms of Marxism, socialism and capitalism are competing for the allegiance of the people, what social ethic does, or can, Buddhism offer?

Try and grapple with the problem of how Buddhism can offer a message on a social, and not just an individual, level. Choose a problem that is a pressing issue for the people of the world. Examples to consider might be the environment, the role of women, population control, nuclear proliferation or achieving a more equitable distribution of the world's resources. Given your study of Buddhist thought, could Buddhism formulate a social philosophy to deal with the issue you have chosen? Does Buddhism have a social dimension, or is it concerned only with individual salvation? Does Buddhist thought contain criteria for evaluating social issues (i.e.."what is fair", "what is equitable","what is moral")? If so, what might be these criteria? How could these criteria be applied to the particular issue you are considering?

PART EIGHT AN ESSAY FOR DEEPER CONSIDERATION

Essay Question

Compare the views of Self (Atman) presented in the Upanishads and in Early Buddhism. Delineate and examine the arguments and justifications given by both sides to support their positions. How would you evaluate the soundness of each side's argument?

Tips for Answering

This essay question asks you to develop your essay by reasoning in ways similar to previous "Deeper Consideration" essays. For example, you are clearly being asked to compare (and contrast) the Upanishadic view of Atman to the Buddhist view of Atman. In order to undertake such a comparison you will have to describe the basic positions of the two traditions as you understand them. In addition, you will have to analyze the positions of each to be able to delineate their arguments. Nevertheless, in one sense, this question is asking you to go beyond merely comparing two positions, or analyzing the significance of each position. It is asking for a critique, or evaluation, of each position. That is to say, you are being asked to lay out the arguments on each side of this issue, and then evaluate which, if either, side is presenting a sound argument or a strong justification.

An argument, in ordinary speech, often means a dispute, or a situation in which two people exchange angry words. But in philosophy and many academic disciplines an argument is a special use of language and reason. Many times when we are speaking or writing we make claims that something is true, or assert that such and such is the case. When we do this we are making assertions, or making truth-claims. When someone advances an argument, however, he or she is not just making assertions. He is also asserting that some of these assertions are reasons for others. That is to say, an argument makes the claim that one or more specific assertions ought to be accepted as true, or probably true, just because certain other statements are true. The goal of an argument, therefore, is to get you to accept one assertion as being true by showing you that other assertions are true. Seen in this way the minimal ingredients of an argument are: 1) at least one statement that is reasoned *for* (this is the *conclusion*), 2) at least one statement that is alleged to *support* the conclusion (this is the *reason*), and 3) some signal that an argument is taking place (the use of terms such as "therefore" or "because").

The above essay question is asking you to present, not just the positions of both traditions, but their arguments. You will need to present not just the conclusions that each side takes, but also what reasons, evidence or justification each gives for believing the conclusion to be true. When you are presenting the argument for each side, you should attempt to do so fairly and objectively. You are also being asked, however, to evaluate the arguments or the evidence. Does the evidence justify the conclusion? When you undertake such an evaluation you will probably argue much more in favor of one of the positions. Make sure that in answering this question you are not just giving your opinion, but are taking a position based on rigorous examination of the arguments. You are taking your own position and backing it up; which is to say, you are advancing your own argument.

PART NINE PROJECTS FOR DEVELOPING RELIGIOUS EMPATHY

1. The Buddha claimed to have discovered a number of significant truths concerning the nature of human existence, and the path to a resolution of the fundamental human problem. One of these truths was the realization that all composite existence is transitory (*anicca* in Pali, *mujô* in Japanese.) People think there is a stability in their lives that the Buddhists claim does not really exist. If we look closely at ourselves and the world around us we will see impermanence, not stability.

This idea of change is reflected in many Buddhist writings. Consider this poem written by a medieval Japanese Buddhist monk:

When we consider the self, it is like a bubble on the water;
After it has burst, there is no one there.

When we reflect on our lives, they are like the reflections of the moon;
As unstaying as the rise and the fall of the breath.

Even though we cherish the beneficial forms of gods and men;
No one can retain them.

Even though we hate the agony of being hungry ghosts and beasts;
After all, these forms are easy to take on. . .

The smelling of scents, the savoring of tastes,
Are for a brief period only.

When the operations of the breath cease,
No functions stay behind in the body.

From far, far back in the distant past
Until today, until this instant,

Because all the things we have thought we wanted
Have not been granted, we suffer.[4]

Try to share the Buddhist way of viewing the world by examining the impermanence in ourselves and the world. What within yourself is permanent and unchanging? Is it your body? Examine how your body changes during the course of time: you lose skin cells and hair, you lose or gain weight, you become older and slower. Maybe your consciousness is permanent? Examine then your thoughts. Do your thoughts stay still and are they constant? Try focusing on one thought for a minute or two. Do you discover that your thoughts are constantly changing, shifting rapidly from one thought to another which replaces it? Do you find that the emotions are more permanent? You might find that the feeling you awake with only lasts a few minutes. Each feeling is soon replaced by another feeling. This is the point of the Buddhist analysis: that when we closely examine ourselves we see that there is no permanence, only change. Does this mean that there is nothing here? The Buddhists would also reject this option. It is not that there is nothing, just that what there is is dynamic and changing. Of course, many Hindus disagreed with the Buddhists on this point. For the Hindus there is something permanent that underlies all the change. When you analyze who you are, do you see a permanent Self as the Hindus thought? Whose analysis seems more accurate?

2. The Buddhist links the idea of impermanence to the idea of the composite nature of things. Things change because they are not really objects, but are parts in an interdependent relationship with a linguistical overlay. As Nagasena says to King Milinda, the word "chariot" is nothing but a convenient designation for the axle, banner, wheel, etc. in a certain causal relationship to each other. We think we live in a world of objects, but the Buddhists tell us we are wrong.

   Try one more bit of Buddhist analysis. Choose any object you can see. What do you mean when you call it an object? Is it one thing or a group of parts joined together? How could you analyze it into smaller parts? Now, choose any one of those smaller parts. Is it not the case that this part is itself made up of still smaller parts? Do we still not have a group of parts? Now, you can choose one of those smaller parts, and start the analysis again. You can see where this process is leading. Either you must eventually reach a part so small it can not be subdivided, or this analysis must proceed on an infinite course. The Buddhists claim that this process does reach an end, which is when one reaches the smallest possible unit of time and space (<u>dharmas</u>). Does your analysis lead you to see the Buddhist point of view? What might we call these smallest parts today?

3. Much of the Buddhist teaching is expressed in fairly abstract or analytical thought. It is perhaps for this reason that Buddhism has also expressed its teaching in a more concrete manner: art. The story of the Buddha's life was expressed in sculpture and in painting. Each Buddhist culture took the same basic motifs and expressed them in a slightly different manner. Much of this rich harvest of Buddhist art is available for viewing in this country.

If you are fortunate enough to be near a museum with a good collection of Asian art, get together with a friend and take a trip to the museum. Observe if the museum has art from any of the major countries influenced by Buddhism: India, Sri Lanka, Tibet, China, Korea, Japan and the Southeast Asian countries. Which of these collections contain art with Buddhist figures and themes? How can you tell if the art is in some sense "Buddhist?" What might have been the original function of these objects? Can you find two objects from different countries (for example, India and China) that deal with the same theme (for example, two statues of Sakyamuni Buddha or two paintings of the life of the Buddha?) What are the differences in the two objects? What factors (cultural, historical) might explain the different treatments? What aspects of the Buddhist world view can you see expressed in art?

ANSWER KEY TO SELF-TEST SECTION

B) Multiple Choice

1. c	6. b
2. c	7. a
3. d	8. b
4. c	9. a
5. d	10. d

C) True-False

1. T	6. T
2. F	7. T
3. T	8. F
4. F	9. F
5. T	10. T

Notes

[1]Satasahasrika XLV:119, Buddhist Texts Through the Ages, ed. Edward Conze et al., trans. Edward Conze (New York: Harper Torchbooks, 1964) 153.

[2]Tannishô, words attributed to Shinran Shônin, Chap. 1., unpublished translation by the author, David C. Prejsnar.

[3]Buddhaghosa, Visuddhi-Magga, XVI, Buddhism In Translation, ed. tran. Henry Clarke Warren (1896, New York: Antheneum, 1968) 146.

[4]Ippen Shônin, Betsuganwasan, tran. David C. Prejsnar, "Ippen's View of Time and Temporality in the Betsuganwasan", Jishûshi Kenkyû 1.1 (1985): 6-7.

Chapter 5
Jainism and Sikhism

PART ONE LEARNING OBJECTIVES

Doing these exercises, in conjunction with reading the textbook, should help you to achieve the following objectives. Read them and see how many you already have mastered; then study the following terms and concepts, and work through the exercises. After you have completed all the exercises, return to this section and review the objectives again.

You should be able to:

1. Name the two major orders of Jain monks, and delineate the main points of disagreement between the two orders.

2. Give the life story of the twenty-fourth Tirthankara, Mahavira, illustrating how his life exemplified Jain teachings, and explain how the two major orders differ in presenting the story of Mahavira's life.

3. Name the chief divisions of the Jain scripture, and briefly explain the nature and present status of each of these divisions.

4. Discuss and write about the Jain Worldview; in particular, the Jain view of the Absolute, the relative truth of all views, the universe, the human role in the universe, the fundamental problem and resolution for human beings,

rituals and symbols, community and ethics, and other religious traditions.

5. Explain the Jain concept of <u>ahimsa</u>, and critique and evaluate the Jain justification for their belief in <u>ahimsa</u>.

7. Discuss and analyze the historical background to the founding of the Sikh movement, and discuss in what sense this background may have influenced the Sikh movement and teaching.

8. Give the life story of Guru Nanak, illustrating how his life exemplified Sikh teaching.

9. Discuss and analyze the teachings of Guru Nanak, in particular explaining his view of the Absolute and his view of Hinduism and Islam.

10. Name at least four Sikh gurus who followed Nanak, give a brief outline of their lives, and explain the development of the Sikh movement during their lifetimes.

11. Discuss the view of scripture as it is presented in Sikhism, and consider how this view of scripture compares with the view of scripture in other Indian religious traditions.

12. Discuss and write about the Sikh Worldview; in particular, the Sikh view of the Absolute, humans and the world, the fundamental problem and resolution for human beings, rituals and symbols, community and ethics, life after death and other religious traditions.

13. Describe the current situation for Sikhs in India, and the problem of relations between Sikhs and other religio-ethnic groups in India.

PART TWO TERMS AND INDIVIDUALS

JAINISM

A) <u>Terms and Concepts</u>

Jainism (Jain)	Tirthankaras
Digambara	Shvetambara

"sky clad"
Shakra
householder
moksha
jina
Agama
Parshva
non-jiva (ajiva)
triloka
mohaniya
darshanavaraniya
vedaniya
ayu
gunasthana
Sthanakvasis
asteya
aparigraph
karma
ahimsa
Rshabha
Nirvana
ishatpragbhara
Ardhamagadhi
jivas
loka
samsara
jnanavaraniya
antaraya
nama
gotra
puja
asatya
Brahmacharya
sallekhana

B) Individuals

Mahavira
Jnatrputra Vardhamana
Rshabhadatta
Yashodhara
Indrabhuti Gautama
Haribhadra
Rshabha
Trishala
Siddhartha
Devananda
Priyadarshana
Jinasena
Prince Shreyamsa

C) Texts

Agama
Anga
Acaranga
The Story of Samaraditya
Purva
Angabahya
Great Legend (Mahapurana)

SIKHISM

A) Terms and Concepts

Golden Temple of Amritsar
Guru
Nirguna Brahman
samsara
the Khalsa
Kesh
Kach
Kirpan
NAM
bhais
Sikhism
karma
Saguna Brahman
Hakum
Singh
Kangha
Kara
Adi Granth
gurdwara
nihangs

reincarnation
naya

B) Individuals

Nanak
Tripta
Sulakhani
Angad
Ram Das
Har Gobind
Harkishan
Gobind Rai (Gobind Singh)
Kalu
Hardial
Mardana
Amar Das
Arjan
Har Rai
Teg Bahadur
Singh Bhindranwale

C) Texts

Janam-Sakhi
Japji
Adi Granth
Rahat Maryada

JAINISM AND SIKHISM

D) Individuals and Terms From Other Traditions

Hinduism
Buddha
Kshatriyas
Mohandas K. Gandhi
Islam
Muhammad
yogins
Dravidian
Kabir
Veda
Buddhism
Brahmins
Shiva
Brahman-Atman
Akbar
Sufis
Aryan
Sant
Vishnu
Quran

PART THREE GUIDED REVIEW

1. The two heterodox religious traditions, besides Buddhism, that have been very influential in India are ________________ and ________________________.

2. In Jainism the term "Tirthankara" means those who are ________________________.

3. ____________________ was the historical founder of Jainism and the ______________________ in the line of Tirthankaras.

4. The two major orders of Jain monks are the ______________________ and the _______________________.

5. The order that rejects the wearing of clothes and does not allow women to become members of the religious order is ______________________________.

6. The order that believes that Mahavira was conceived through an embryo transfer is ___________________________.

7. For some Jains not wearing clothes is important because it indicates that the monk __________________________________.

8. When Mahavira had achieved Nirvana he became known as a "jina", which means _______________. A follower of a jina is called a ________________.

9. The name for the Jain canon, or collection of scripture, is _______________________. It is divided into categories.

10. A cornerstone of the Jain philosophy is that no doctrine can claim to have _____________________. Thus, doctrines are knowledge from a particular standpoint (nayas) which is relative, but from some point of view all doctrines have some _____________________.

11. Concerning the idea of The Absolute, Jainism denies that there is a _________________.

12. The Jains conceive of the universe as be comprised of two categories: _____________________ and _______________________.

13. Jiva could be defined as _______________________________.

14. For Jainism, the "glue" that binds jiva to ajiva, humans to samsara is _______________________.

15. Three requirements which embody the Jain principles of reverence for life and detachment from physical things are ________________, ________________, and __________________.

16. Three practices which Jains might engage in would be _________________________, __________________________, and __________________________.

17. ________________________ is the Jain doctrine of non-violence and respect for life. The modern Hindu leader who attributed his practice of non-violence to the Jains was ______________________________.

18. The youngest of the major religions of India is ______________________.

19. Some scholars see this Indian religion being very influenced by ____________________________. Sikhs, however, would reject the idea that ___________________________.

20. ____________ is seen by some scholars as a forerunner of the Sikh movement in that he would _____________________. Sikhs would ______________ this idea.

21. The actual founder of the Sikh movement and the first guru in the lineage of gurus was ________________________.

22. Nanak is famous for stating that "There is no __________ and no ________________________", which means that ________ ____.

23. In comparing Nanak's views with that of Hinduism, he agreed with Hinduism in ____________________________________ _____________________________, but he disagreed with Hinduism in ____.

24. It could be said that the central teaching of Nanak is that ____.

25. Nanak's view of the human soul and its relation with God is ____ ____.

26. Nanak saw the Word of God as ____________________________ ____________________________________.

27. Nanak saw five stages in an individual's progress towards God. A brief summary of these five stages would be:

a)____.
b)____.
c)____.
d)____.
e)____.

28. The successor to Nanak and the second guru was _____________.

29. The guru who began the construction at Amritsar, and under whom the Sikh order began to grow financially prosper was ____________________, who was the ____________ guru.

30. The guru who began to construct the ____________________ at Amritsar and who was tortured to death by Jahangir was ____________________, the ________________ guru.

31. Because of what happened to his father, Har Gobind responded by ______________________________ and by ____.

32. The tenth and last earthly guru was Gobind Rai. He is better known, however, as ____________________________.

33. The Sikh ritual called Khalsa could be described as ____. The five men who first underwent this ritual were called ________________, which means ____________________________.

34. Since the death of the tenth guru the only guru for the Sikhs is ____.

35. The attitude of Sikhism towards the Hindu Brahman and the Muslim Allah is ____.

36. God, for the Sikhs, is both ___________________ and _______________ .

37. If one entered a gurdwara, at the center one would probably find _______________________.

38. At a gurdwara, one might encounter two different types of Sikh functionaries: ________________, who are ______________, and _________________, who are _____________________.

39. In India today, many Sikhs are agitating for the creation of ____.

PART FOUR ANALYZING TEXTS

Below are two texts that were not in the textbook. The texts, however, do contain ideas and concepts with which you should be familiar after reading the textbook and studying the selections in the textbook from primary religious documents. Read each text carefully, compare it to the primary documents you have studied and try to analyze each by answering the following questions: What are the main ideas in the text? What viewpoint or viewpoints might the author of the text represent? Is it possible to identify the specific thinker, discipline, movement, tradition or work from which the text derives? What intellectual, literary, social, cultural or historical influences are reflected in the text? For each of your conclusions, try to point to specific evidence in the text (e.g. terms, ideas, arguments, writing style, etc.) which supports your conclusion. Be careful that your conclusions do not exceed the evidence upon which they rest.

TEXT ONE

There is but one God whose name is True, the Creator, devoid of fear and enmity, immortal, unborn, self-existent, great and bountiful.

The True One was in the beginning, the True One was in the primal age.

The True One is, was, O Nanak, and the True One also shall be. [1]

TEXT TWO

Right belief, right knowledge, right conduct - these together constitute the path to liberation.

Belief in things ascertained as they are is right belief.

This is attained by intuition or understanding.

The categories (_tattvas_) are souls (_jiva_), non-souls, inflow (_asrava_) of karmic matter into the self, bondage (_bandha_) of self by karmic matter, stoppage (_samvara_) of inflow of karmic matter into the self, shedding (_nirjara_) of karmic matter by the self, and liberation (_moksa_) of the self from matter. . .

The points of view (_naya_) are: figurative, general, distributive, actual, descriptive, specific, and active.

Naya may be distinguished from _niksepa_. _Niksepa_ is an aspect of the thing itself. _Naya_ is a point of view from which we make some statement about the thing . . . [2]

PART FIVE SELF-TEST

A) Definitions and Descriptions - Write your own definition or description of each of the following terms, individuals or texts. After completing the self-test, check your answer with the definition or description given in the textbook.

1. ahimsa ____.

2. Singh ____.

3. Sant ____.

4. Jain ____.

5. Guru ____.

6. "sky clad" ____.

7. Adi Granth ____.

8. bhais ____.

9. Digambaras ____.

10. jivas ____.

B) Multiple Choice

1. The Muslim figure who first tried to combine Hinduism and Islam was

   a. Nanak
   b. Mardana
   c. Mahavira
   d. Kabir

2. Which is not one of the five K's of the Singhs?

   a. Comb
   b. Turban
   c. Short pants
   d. Sword.

3. Which of the following religious traditions did not believe in reincarnation?

   a. Jainism
   b. Neither Jainism or Sikhism
   c. Sikhism
   d. Both Jainism and Sikhism

4. The Jain scripture of which eleven of the twelve books are still in existence is the

   a. Purvas
   b. Angas
   c. Angabahya
   d. Vedas

5. Which of the following is not one of the worlds of the Triloka?

   a. The realm of hells
   b. The Middle World
   c. The realm of liberated souls
   d. The realm of The Creator

6. Sikhism began in the

   a. Fifteenth Century C.E.
   b. Sixteen Century C.E.
   c. Fourteenth Century C.E.
   d. Tenth Century C.E

7. Which Sikh guru first took a military stand against the Hindu or Muslim rulers?

   a. Har Gobind
   b. Amar Das
   c. Gobind Singh
   d. Nanak

8. The name of the Jain sect who reject the wearing of clothes is

   a. Digambaras
   b. Shvetambaras
   c. Sautantrikas
   d. Sthanakvavis

9. Which religion in this chapter could be considered monotheistic?

   a. Jainism
   b. Sikhism
   c. Neither
   d. Jainism and Sikhism

10. Which of the following beliefs did Jainism <u>not</u> share with Hinduism?

   a. Karma
   b. Soul
   c. Reincarnation
   d. Authority of Vedas

C) <u>True-False</u>

T F 1. Jains believe that all statements are relative, and can be seen as true from at least one perspective.

T F 2. Sikhs consider the story of Kabir part of their history.

T F 3. The Digambara sect tells a fascinating story of an embryo transfer.

T F 4. The guards at a Sikh gurdwara are the <u>bhais</u>.

T F 5. The Jains have a strong belief in a creator God.

T F 6. The Jain concept of non-violence is termed <u>asatya</u>.

T F 7. According to Jain belief, the Tirthankaras are above the gods.

T F 8. The story of the five blind men and the elephant may be used to illustrate the Jain idea of <u>nayas.</u>

T F 9. Nanak rejected any distinction between Hindu Brahman and Islam's Allah.

T F 10. The guru in Sikhism today is Har Gobind.

PART SIX ESSAY AND DISCUSSION QUESTIONS

1. Define the concept of "ahimsa" and explain its role in Jainism. What reasons might Jainism offer to justify their belief in non-violence?

2. Explain the Jain doctrine of the relativity of all views (<u>naya</u>). How might the Jains use this doctrine to examine and critique the Hindu-Buddhist debate concerning the Atman?

3. Appraise Sikhism as an attempt to transcend the distinction between Hinduism and Islam. Did Sikhism attempt to unify the two religions, and ,if so, did it fail?

4. Write a dialogue between a Jain and a Sikh in which each gives his or her view of armed struggle and the use of violence. What arguments might each side put forward? What, in your view, are the strengths and weaknesses of each position?

PART SEVEN CONFRONTING QUESTIONS AND ISSUES

The religions you have studied up until this chapter have often been the dominant religions within their culture. The two religions discussed in this chapter are different; each of them has, for most of its existence, been a minority religion. In the India of today, both of these religions claim many fewer participants than either Hinduism or Islam. This fact raises an interesting problem: what roles does a religious tradition play when it is a minority belief in a dominant culture?

Imagine that you are a member of a religious community that is a minority belief in a dominant culture. Consider what problems and challenges you might face in this position. You might want to think of other traditions included in the textbook that you may have already studied (Zoroastrianism perhaps). You also might want to think about situations in the world where one area has a dominant religious group and at least one minority faith (Northern Ireland, the former Yugoslavia, India.) What is the current situation in each of these areas? How would you describe relations between the dominant religious group and the minority group(s)? Has each tradition managed to learn and interact peacefully with the others? How has each of these traditions managed to survive and prosper? What historical factors have contributed to the relationship between the different traditions? What approach did each tradition take in order to assure its survival? You might want to consider such factors as organizational structure, clan or tribe loyalty, initiation ceremonies, and political moves. What does your study show you about how dominant and minority religious traditions interact? What examples could be seen as role models, and what examples show the problems with such interaction?

PART EIGHT AN ESSAY QUESTION FOR DEEPER CONSIDERATION

Essay Question

The two religions discussed in this chapter each take interesting positions in regard to the status of truth-claims. Jainism takes the position that all truth-claims are relative. Sikhism could be seen as the attempt to present a valid truth-claim in order to correct two invalid, but opposing, truth-claims (Islam and Hinduism). In an essay, examine the way in which each of these two religions makes claims about what is true, and how these claims illustrate each religions' theory of truth-claims.

Tips For Answering

This is a very complex essay assignment that will require

a great deal of thought and planning. Some suggestions on how you can tackle this assignment will be discussed shortly. But the complexity of the issue makes a discussion of another topic relevant: the thesis statement.

Any good essay needs a clearly formulated and communicated thesis. But when you are tackling a very complex subject it is even more crucial to clearly formulate and state your thesis, or else you, and your reader, run the risk of getting lost in the essay. A thesis can be defined as the general point you want to prove or argue for in your essay. In most essays you will be referring to many specific historical facts, religious doctrines, or view of scholars. These particulars should be included in your essay, however, only because they lend support or clarification to your thesis. Woody Allen once said he became a better director when he learned to leave more jokes on the cutting-room floor. In the same way, too much information or too many arguments can clutter your essay. You need to understand what major point you want to prove and then structure your essay so all the particulars lend support to this thesis.

Before you formulate the thesis for your essay you may need to do some preliminary brainstorming. One topic you should consider is the definition of "truth-claim." The essay question uses this term but does not define it. Many philosophers use this term, so you might want to consult a dictionary or encyclopedia of philosophy to become acquainted with their discussion of the term. The general meaning of the term, however, is to make a claim that something is true, or something is so and so. It is to take a position about what is true, and what is not true.

Begin your answer by breaking the essay question into smaller units. The first question is "What type of claims does each religion make?" You might want to give a few examples of the type of claim each religion makes. You would want to analyze these to see if there is anything distinctive about the claims. Does one tradition make one type of claim (maybe, moral claims), while another tradition focuses on a different type (ritual claims, for example.) Another possibility might be to analyze the same type of claim in both traditions; for example, you could isolate the claims that each religion makes concerning the Absolute. Is there something unique, for example, in the logic of the Jain claim concerning the Absolute? If you choose this approach you would be focusing on the structure of the claims, not on the content of the claims.

The second part of the assignment asks you to step back and examine what you have discovered in each religion. Are the type of claims each religious tradition makes an indication of a more general approach to truth? For example, if a religion were to say that the Absolute could truthfully be described in two, apparently contradictory, ways, what would this show about that tradition's general theory of truth? If a religious tradition thought that the Absolute was totally beyond any linguistic assertions, what would this show about that tradition's general theory of truth? To come full circle, your conclusions concerning the theories of truth embedded in the different traditions would, most probably, form the basis for your overall thesis statement.

PART NINE PROJECTS FOR DEVELOPING RELIGIOUS EMPATHY

1. One of the most distinctive teachings of India is the Jain reverence for life (ahimsa). The Jains believe that no living thing should be destroyed or harmed. Many individuals from other religious traditions respect the Jains for stressing the value of life and the idea of non-violence. Sometimes, however, these same people believe that the Jains take their beliefs to an extreme.

   You might try to practice for one day the Jain ideal of ahimsa. But this might turn out to be rather difficult. Rather, try to consider how you would have to live if you did practice ahimsa in this manner. Start by considering your clothing; what type of clothes could you wear if you did not want to harm any life? Would you have to walk around naked, as the Digambaras sect does? Could you wear wool or cotton clothes? What kind of shoes could you wear? Consider what type of food you could eat. Could you eat meat or fish? Would eggs or diary products be acceptable? Could an argument be made against even vegetables or grain? Finally, think about how we move around. Would driving a car be allowed, since many animals and insects are killed by cars? Would any form of locomotion be acceptable? Could not even walking result in stepping on ants or insects? In conclusion, you might want to consider whether anybody could follow the path of ahimsa in a Western environment?

ANSWER KEY TO SELF-TEST

B) Multiple Choice

1. d	6. b
2. b	7. a
3. d	8. a
4. b	9. b
5. d	10. d

C) True-False

1. T	6. F
2. F	7. T
3. F	8. T
4. F	9. T
5. F	10. F

Notes

[1]*The Sikh Religion; Its Gurus, Sacred Writings and Anthems*, ed. M. A. MacAuliffe, vol. 1 (Oxford: Clarendon Press, 1909) 35.

[2]Sri Umasvati Acarya, *Tattvarthadhigama Sutra*, in *A Sourcebook in Indian Philosophy*, ed. Sarvepalli Radhakrishnan et al., trans. J. L. Jaini (Princeton, N.J.: Princeton University Press, 1957) 252-253.

PART THREE
Religions of China and Japan

PART ONE LEARNING OBJECTIVES

Doing these exercises, in conjunction with reading the textbook, should help you to achieve the following objectives. Read them and see how many you already have mastered; then study the following terms and concepts, and work through the exercises. After you have completed all the exercises, return to this section and review the objectives again.

You should be able to:

1. Identify and explain some theoretical constructs concerning how the family of religions in China and Japan are different from the family of religions in India.

2. Explain generally the role "harmony" has played in Chinese religion, and give at least three examples of symbols of harmony or activities which maintain harmony.

3. Explain briefly the role of "harmony" in Shinto, and how the Japanese saw Shinto's relation to religions not native to Japan.

PART TWO TERMS AND INDIVIDUALS

A) Terms and Concepts

Dao
Yin
Earth
Daoism
Yang
Heaven
Kami
Confucianism

B) Individuals and Terms From Other Traditions

Mahayana Buddhism
Theravada Buddhism

PART THREE GUIDED REVIEW

1. In general, one might say that the religions in India emphasized ______________________________, while religions that arose in China and Japan tended to emphasize ______________________________.

2. Mahayana Buddhism was accepted by the Chinese and Japanese because it presented a view of ______________________.

3. Some scholars believe that the concept of ________ never fully developed in China as it did in the West.

4. The concept of harmony with ______________ or harmony within the ____________________ are found in China, but not typically the idea of harmony within ____________.

5. In China the concept of the ____________ symbolized harmony and the source of __________ and __________. Another duality that symbolized harmony was the concepts of ________ and ________ .

6. In Japanese religion extraordinary powers in the natural or the human realm are termed __________. The native Japanese way which centers around these is called _________.

7. The Japanese, in general, came to believe that non-native religions such as _________, __________, or _________, could _____________ their native religious practices.

PART FOUR QUESTIONS FOR CONSIDERATION

As you study the religions of China and Japan, and read Part III of the textbook try to reflect upon, and even write out, responses to the following questions. These questions are designed to help you synthesize what you are learning about Chinese and Japanese religions, and reach your own conclusions concerning the significance of these traditions.

1. The textbook claims that the religions of China and Japan should be considered a "family of religions" because they share certain characteristics. What are these characteristics? Can you identify any other shared characteristics besides the ones mentioned in the book?

2. Based on your study of the religions of China and those of Japan, would you agree that these religions all belong in the same "family"? What are some of the characteristics that Shinto shares with the religions of China? In what ways is Shinto different from the religions that originated in China?

3. Mahayana Buddhism did not originate in either China or Japan, but attracted many followers in both countries. What elements might Buddhism have been able to contribute to the universes of Chinese and Japanese religions? How might the worldviews of China and Japan have played a role in reshaping Chinese and Japanese Buddhism?

4. Having studied Indian religion, try to compare the central characteristics of Indian religion to those of Japanese and Chinese religions.

Chapter 6
Religions of China and Japan

PART ONE LEARNING OBJECTIVES

Doing these exercises, in conjunction with reading the textbook, should help you to achieve the following objectives. Read them and see how many you already have mastered; then study the following terms and concepts, and work through the exercises. After you have completed all the exercises, return to this section and review the objectives again.

You should be able to:

1. Describe the native Chinese beliefs, rituals and texts that formed the background to the thought of Confucius and Laozi.

2. Explain what historical evidence regarding the lives of Laozi and Zhuangzi, the date and authorship of the Dao De Jing and the early historical development of Daoist philosophy.

3. Delineate and analyze in both discussion and writing the thought of the Dao De Jing and the Zhuangzi, and, in particular, their view of the Dao, human nature, the nature and role of the Sage, the relation of the individual to nature, and the relation of the individual to society.

4. Explain what is meant by religious, sectarian Daoism, and how this movement compares with the type of Daoism seen in the Dao De Jing and the Zhuangzi.

5. Name and describe at least two Daoist contemplation techniques, and show how these illustrate Daoist meditation.

6. Describe the historical situation during the latter Zhou dynasty and relate this situation to the life of Confucius.

7. Delineate and analyze in both discussion and writing the thought of Confucius, and, in particular, his views concerning human nature, the nature and role of the Junzi, propriety (li) and benevolence (ren), and the relation of the individual to society.

8. Name at least two native Chinese schools of thought, besides the Daoists, who challenged Confucius's outlook, and give a brief description of the basic positions of each school.

9. Describe the basic course of development of Confucianism after Confucius, and give a brief description of the positions of at least three Confucian thinkers.

10. Define what is meant by Chinese folk religion and discuss some of its practices and worldviews.

11. Discuss and write about the Daoist and Confucian Worldview, in particular, contrasting and comparing their views of the Absolute, the universe, the human role in the universe, the fundamental problem and resolution for human beings, community and ethics, and rituals and symbols.

12. Show the importance of education in the Confucian Worldview, and illustrate how this aspect of Confucianism may have a continued influence in China and in other East Asian societies.

13. Discuss the native Japanese view of man, nature and kami, and illustrate how aspects of this view is manifested in at least two myths preserved in the Kojiki, in ritual and in history.

14. Describe the basic course of development of Shinto from the time of Prince Shôtoku Taishi up through the Second World War. In particular, describe the changing

relationship between Shinto and Buddhism.

15. Define and give illustrations of State Shinto, Shrine Shinto and Sectarian Shinto, including a discussion of the three major classifications of Sectarian Shinto.

16. Discuss and give examples of two "New Religions" that have developed out of Shinto, and indicate the general characteristics and role of these new religions.

17. Discuss and write about the Shinto Worldview, in particular, the Shinto view of the Absolute, the universe, the human role in the universe, the fundamental problem and resolution for human beings, community and ethics, rituals and symbols, and Shinto's relationship with other religions.

18. Analyze and write about the role of patriotism in Shinto and Japanese history, and the challenges in this area to contemporary Shinto.

PART TWO TERMS AND INDIVIDUALS

A) CHINA

a) <u>Terms and Concepts</u>

Daoism
Confucianism
Xia dynasty
Shang dynasty
Zhou dynasty
Son of Heaven
Dao
Yang
Yin
Heaven
Earth
wuwei
Shang Di
the Jade Emperor (Yu Huang)
Ling Bao
Zaoshen
Three Purities
embryonic breathing (taixi)
shouyi
junzi
li
yi
zhongyong (the mean)
ren
shu (reciprocity)
Tianming (Mandate of Heaven)
Mohist School
Fajia School (Legalists)
Han dynasty
Neo-Confucianism
chi
Taiji
shih
ju
Chinese folk religion
ancestors
hungry ghosts
poe

b) Individuals

Laozi
Zhuangzi
Ge Hong
Confucius (Kongfuzi)
Mozi
Kuan Chung
Han Feizi
Mencius (Mengzi)
Xunzi
Zhuxi
Sun Yat-sen
Chiang K'ai Shek
Mao Zedong

c) Texts

Yijing
Dao De Ching
Baopuzi
Li Ji
Five Classics
Shujing
Shijing
Ch'un Ch'iu
Four Books
Analects (LunYu)
The Great Learning
The Doctrine of the Mean
The Book of Mencius
Shiji
The Zhuangzi

d) Individuals and Terms from Other Traditions

Heraclitus
Niccolo Machiavelli
Aristotle
Buddha
Thomas Aquinas

B) JAPAN

a) Terms and Concepts

Shinto (kami no michi)
torii
kami
shaman
miko (Shrine maiden)
Izanagi
Izanami
Yomi
Amaterasu
Susanoo
Tsukiyomi
Okunushi
Ninigi
bushido
harakiri (seppaku)
shôgun
state Shinto
sectarian Shinto
Ise Shrine
kami-dana
Shinto Taikyô
Izumo ôyashirokyô
Shinto Shuseiha
Shinto Taiseikyô
Shinshukyô
Honchi Taishin
Shinrikyô
Ontakekyô
Fusokyô
Sengen Daishin
Jikkokyô
Kurozumikyô
konjin
Konkokyô

Misogikyô
ômoto
P. L. Kyôdan
norito
saisei itchi
misogi harai
Tenri-kyô/Honmichi
Seichô-no-le
yamabushi

b) <u>Individuals</u>

Emperor Jimmu (legendary)
Emperor Shômu
Toyotomi Hideyoshi
Emperor Shôwa (Hirohito)
Kurozumi Munetada
Inoue Masakane
Onisaburo
Miki Tokuchika
Prince Shôtoku Taishi
Oda Nobunaga
Emperor Meiji
Yoshimura Masamochi
Kawate Bunjiro (Konko Daijin)
Deguchi Nao
Miki Nakayama
Taniguchi Masaharu

c) <u>Texts</u>

Kojiki
Nihongi

d) <u>Individuals and Terms from Other Traditions</u>

Commodore Matthew C. Perry
Zen Buddhism
Kokubun-ji temples
butsudan

PART THREE GUIDED REVIEW

1. Among the major religions studied in this chapter _____________ and ____________were originally Chinese, while _______________ is distinctively Japanese.

2. The earliest Chinese dynasty for which there is historical evidence is the ______________ dynasty, whose dates were from __________ to ___________.

3. The dynasty during which Confucius lived was the ______________ dynasty, whose dates were from __________ to ___________.

4. The Chinese believe that two forces are at work in the universe. The light and active force is termed ____________. The dark and passive force is termed _____________.

5. These two balancing forces are often correlated with another pair of terms: ____________ and _____________.

6. The ________________ is an ancient text which uses sixty-four hexagrams and has been used for thousands of years by the Chinese for guidance and divination.

7. The beginnings of Daoism is usually ascribed to the possibly legendary figure, _____________, who is credited with writing the text called the ______________________.

8. Daoists tend to emphasize not society, but ________________. They argue that the best course to follow to achieve harmony is the _________________ course.

9. For Laozi "the door of all subtleties", that which a person should be in harmony with, is termed the __________.

10. The Daoists argue that one should act without acting. This Daoist concept is that of ____________. An example a Daoist might give of this principle is _________________.

11. The second major Daoist thinker was _________________.

12. Religious Daoism was another form of Daoism that developed in China; it devoted its attention to such activities as ________________ and ___________________.

13. The form of Daoism which developed temples and attempted to compete organizationally with Buddhism is termed ___________________________.

14. For Daoism the best lifestyle is one that is ___________ and ______________.

15. One criticism that a Confucian might level against the Daoist would be that ____________________________ ______________.

16. "Embryonic breathing" (taixi) is _____________ ____.

17. Confucius did not claim to present innovative ideas, but rather claimed to present ideas that he believed were from ______________________.

18. The condition of China during Confucius's lifetime can be described as one of ___________________________________ ____.

19. During his lifetime Confucius traveled throughout China in search of ______________________________________.

20. While The Analects are not definitive on this point, it has been argued that Confucius believed that humans were basically __________.

21. Confucius said that the _________________ understood what was moral and was at ease without being arrogant. However, the __________________ understood what was profitable and was arrogant without being at ease.

22. The way things should be done, or appropriateness, is termed in Chinese _____________. When these rules become internalized these are called _____________.

23. Ren could be defined as ________________________________.

24. Mozi's central teaching was that ______________________ ____.

25. Whereas Confucius believed people should ________________ their enemies, Mozi responded that people should ______________ their enemies.

26. Han Feizi was a member of the ____________________ School. This school argued that human nature was _______________.

27. One difference between Han Feizi and Confucius was that Han Feizi believed that the good ruler should govern through _____________________, but Confucius believed the good ruler should govern through _____________________.

28. The Five Classics of Confucianism are: __________________, ______________________, __________________, _________________, and _________________. To these are added the Four Books: ______________________, ___________________, _________________, and __________________.

29. Two influential later Confucianists were Mencius and Xunzi. They differed in their assessment of human nature. Mencius viewed man's nature as basically __________, whereas Xunzi thought man by nature was basically ___________.

30. The great Neo-Confucian thinker Zhuxi concluded that everything comes into being through _________ and ____________.

31. Zhuxi saw ____________________________ as the ultimate principle in the Universe which is behind heaven and earth, behind yin and yang.

32. The Maoist view of Confucianism was that it
____
____.

33. A religion that is understood and practiced by the general population, as differentiated from that which is taught by the scholar and priests, is termed a ____________.

34. Poe are ____.

35. The doctrine that the ruler's authority was derived from heaven, and that he could only continue to receive this authority as long as he cared for the welfare of the people and the state was termed ___________________________.

36. Confucian ethics is based on reciprocity which means
____.

37. The textbook focuses on one area in Chinese society where Confucius and Confucianism had a significant impact; this was
______________________.

38. The term "Shinto" means ___________________.

39. Stunning natural phenomena, extraordinary people or objects, great leaders are all viewed in Shinto as
___________.

40. According to Japanese myth, the islands of Japan were created by ____.

41. In one of the most famous Japanese myths, Susanoo coaxed Amaterasu out of the cave by showing her a ______________.

42. According to many Japanese the kami and the Buddhist bodhisattvas and Buddhas are the ___________________.

43. The code of Bushido reflects elements of
__________________, ________________________ and
______________________.

44. That form of Shinto which stressed the divine origin of Japan, the divinity of the Emperor and the duties of the individual to his country is ________________________.

45. The center for observing reverence for the ancestors in a Japanese house is the ______________________. A Japanese home will also often have a different sanctuary that is Buddhist in nature called a ________________.

46. According to the Japanese Agency for Cultural Affairs, sectarian Shinto can be classified into three groups: 1)__________________________, 2)__________________________, and 3) __________________________.

47. Miki Nakayama founded the New Religion termed ________________. Its Teaching of the Heavenly Reason is the belief that ____________________________________.

48. In Shinto the deity who has been most venerated is ________________________.

49. Denise Lardner Carmody has described the status of Japanese women in terms of the following four roles: as ______________, as ______________, as ______________, and as ________________.

50. The Grand Ise Shrine was often the destination for ____________________.

51. If one visited a Shinto shrine a visitor might typically see a Japanese do the following: ______________________, ______________________, ______________________.

52. Two forms of pilgrimage during the Tokugawa Period were ___________________ and ______________________.

53. Earhart defines the concept of the "Japanese people" to mean ____.

PART FOUR ANALYZING TEXTS

Below are three texts that were not in the textbook. The texts, however, do contain ideas and concepts with which you should be familiar after reading the textbook and studying the selections in the textbook from primary religious documents. Read each text carefully, compare it to the primary documents in the text and try to analyze each by answering the following questions: What are the main ideas in the text? What viewpoint or viewpoints might the author of the text represent? Is it possible to identify the specific thinker, discipline, movement, tradition or work from which the text derives? What intellectual, literary, social, cultural or historical influences are reflected in the text? For each of your conclusions, try to point to specific evidence in the text (e.g. terms, ideas, arguments, writing style, etc.) which supports your conclusion. Be careful that your conclusions do not exceed the evidence upon which they rest.

TEXT ONE

The Master said, "I have transmitted what was taught to me without making up anything of my own. I have been faithful to and loved the Ancients. . . . I have listened in silence and noted what was said, I have never grown tired of learning nor wearied of teaching others what I have learned. . . . The thought that 'I have left my moral order untended, my learning unperfected, that I have heard of righteous men, but have been unable to go to them; have heard of evil men, but have been unable to reform them' - it is these thoughts that disquiet me."[1]

TEXT TWO

The True Way is one and the same, in every country and throughout heaven and earth. This Way, however, has been correctly transmitted only in our Imperial Land. Its transmission in all foreign countries was lost long ago in early antiquity, and many and varied ways have been expounded, each country representing its own way as the Right Way. . . . Let me state briefly what the one original Way is. One must understand, first of all, the universal principle of the world. The principle is that Heaven and earth, all the gods and all phenomena, were brought into existence by the creative spirits of two deities - Takami-musubi and Kami-musubi. The birth of all humankind in all ages and the existence of all things and all matter have been the result of that creative spirit. . . . This spirit of creativity is a miraculously divine act the reason for which is beyond the comprehension of the human intellect.[2]

TEXT THREE

Exterminate the sage, discard the wise
And the people will benefit a hundredfold;
Exterminate benevolence, discard rectitude,
And the people will again be filial;
Exterminate ingenuity, discard profit,
And there will be no more thieves and bandits.
These three, being false adornments, are not enough
And the people must have something to which they
can attach themselves:
Exhibit the unadorned and embrace the uncarved block,
Have little thought of self and as few desires as
possible. [3]

PART FIVE SELF-TEST

a) Definitions and Descriptions - Write your own definition or description of each of the following terms, individuals or texts. After completing the self-test, check your answer with the definition or description given in the textbook.

1. li ______________________________
____
______________________________________.

2. wuwei ______________________________
____
______________________________________.

3. torii ______________________________
____
______________________________________.

4. yin ______________________________
____
______________________________________.

5. bushido ______________________________
____
______________________________________.

6. ren ____
____
____.

7. sectarian Shinto ______________________________
____
____.

8. shouyi ____
____
____.

9. kami ____
____
____.

10. junzi ____
____
____.

b) Multiple Choice

1. Japanese emperors claimed to be descended from the Sun Goddess who was

   a. Susanoo.
   b. Tsukiyomi.
   c. Izanagi.
   d. Amaterasu.

2. The Confucian thinker who argued that man's nature is basically evil is

   a. Mencius.
   b. Confucius.
   c. Xunzi.
   d. Zhuxi.

3. The doctrine that the ruler gets his mandate to rule from heaven and that it is provisional on his governing the state on the basis of benevolence is called

   a. Ren.
   b. Tianming.
   c. Zhongyong.
   d. Tian.

4. Which of the following would best describe the beliefs of Laozi?

   a. The sage should love all people equally.
   b. The sage should try to subdue and regulate nature.
   c. The sage should seek harmony with the Dao.
   d. The sage should seek to always be in accord with li.

5. Which dynasty did Confucius look to for guidance in how to order society and run a government?

   a. Zhou dynasty.
   b. Shang dynasty.
   c. Xia dynasty.
   d. Han dynasty.

6. Which of the following practices is not mentioned as one of the practices of magical Daoism?

   a. embryonic breathing
   b. study of The Great Learning
   c. alchemy
   d. fortune-telling

7. Which of the following would be considered by the Japanese people as a kami?

   a. A famous leader from Japanese history.
   b. A majestic mountain.
   c. An large, old tree.
   d. All of the above.

8. The beginnings of Daoism are usually attributed to

   a. Laozi
   b. Zhuangzi
   c. Han Feizi
   d. Mozi

9. Which of the following is not one of the Five Relations of Confucianism?

   a. Elder brother-younger brother.
   b. Father-son.
   c. Ruler-subject.
   d. Mother-daughter.

10. Which of the following is <u>not</u> used by the Agency for Cultural Affairs as a classification for sectarian Shinto groups?

a. Traditional sects.
b. Mountain worship sects.
c. Nichiren sects.
d. Sects based on revelation.

C. <u>True-False</u>

T F 1. For Chinese people, the Yang and the Yin are seen as balancing each other in the Dao.

T F 2. In the famous Shinto myth, Izanami hid in a cave, and had to be lured out by Susanoo.

T F 3. A Confucian scholar would act by following the principle of wuwei.

T F 4. The Legalist School believed that the ruler should govern his state through severe punishments.

T F 5. In traditional Chinese thought, Yang is believed to be the passive, female, dark force in the universe.

T F 6. Mencius was more concerned with the individual than was Confucius.

T F 7. The earliest dynasty for which there is evidence is the Xia dynasty.

T F 8. State Shinto went through a period of rapid growth following Japan's surrender in 1945.

T F 9. Laozi was elevated to the status of a god in sectarian Daoism.

T F 10. The main activity of the Fusokyô sect is climbing Mt. Fuji.

PART SIX ESSAY AND DISCUSSION QUESTIONS

1. Analyze and compare the Indian worldview, as exemplified by Hinduism and Buddhism, and the Chinese worldview, as exemplified by Daoism and Confucianism.

2. What advice do you think Laozi would give to a ruler? Do you think Laozi's philosophy could be used to govern a country? Why or why not?

3. Confucius is held to have said:

   At 15, I had my mind bent on learning.
   At 30, I stood firm.
   At 40, I had no doubts.
   At 50, I knew the decrees of Heaven.
   At 60, my ear was an obedient organ for the reception of truth.
   At 70, I could follow what my heart desired, without transgressing what was right.

   How does the progression outlined in this quote illustrate Confucius's view of the Superior Man (junji), and how one progresses towards this goal? Would Laozi agree or disagree with this view of the Superior Man, and why?

4. Do you think Confucianism, as it is contained in the writings of Confucius and Mencius, should be categorized as a religion? What is your definition of religion?

5. Some scholars have argued that in Shinto the notion of "pollution" is important, but not the notion of "evil". Using evidence from Japanese myths and Shinto rituals, evaluate the soundness of this statement. What do you think is the difference between the notion of "evil", and that of "pollution"?

6. Describe the different types of Shinto, and discuss how they differ amongst themselves.

PART SEVEN CONFRONTING QUESTIONS AND ISSUES

A) CHINA

In the spring of 1989 a movement for political reform and greater democracy began to spread in the People's

Republic of China. It spread first among Chinese university students, and then among Chinese workers, and peasants. At the center of this movement was a large group of Chinese young people who encamped in Beijing's Gate of Heavenly Peace Square, the symbolic center of the Socialist state. After appearing to tolerate the growth and spread of the movement, the Chinese leadership finally ordered army troops and tanks to clear the square. On June 4, 1989 the troops killed hundreds of the people in or near the square. Thousands of the leaders and members of the democracy movement were hunted down, and put on trial. Some were executed. Many more were sent to prison.

The textbook asks, "How much Confucian influence remains among the Chinese people?" Using the events in the Spring of 1989 as a test case, to what extent can one make a connection between the ancient teachings of China - Confucianism, Daoism and Legalism - and the contemporary political situation? What are the similarities, if any, between the students' ideals of reforming a corrupt political system and achieving greater democracy, and the ideals of the traditional systems? Would any of the traditional Chinese teachings be supportive of democracy? Which, if any, of the schools of thought would have counseled the Chinese government to act as it did? Which, if any, of the schools of thought would have counseled against such a course of action? Finally, does your analysis indicate that the ancient teachings still resonate in modern China, or do the traditional teachings have little relevancy for today's China?

B)JAPAN

World events in the closing years of the Twentieth Century hold promise for a new world order, a new internationalism. The integration of the European market, the increasingly international nature of finance and business, the linking of world communications through satellites and computer networks, and the ending of the Cold War are all factors promoting this new order. Today, a nation and a people who define themselves in terms of a consciousness of nationalism (in Japanese, kokuminshigi) appear to run the danger of being excluded from the new international community.

It is not surprising, therefore, that one of the major topics of debate in Japan is how, and to what degree, Japan should become more "international". Implicit within this debate is a tension within Japanese society between a strong belief in their national uniqueness and a desire to build on what they share with other peoples. As the textbook states, "[Shinto] is so much a part of the ethnic life of Japanese people that it must be included wherever their cultural identity is considered." Given your study of the beliefs and rituals of Shinto, what role, if any, can Shinto play in supporting an international role for Japan? Is Shinto a belief system that tends to only lead the Japanese to an awareness of their national uniqueness? Are their elements within Shinto that can also help the Japanese to define a new international consciousness? What might be these elements, if they exist?

PART EIGHT AN ESSAY FOR DEEPER CONSIDERATION

Essay Question

You are the Emperor of China. A group of dedicated political activists have barricaded themselves, along with a number of hostages, in a house in the capital. The group claims that you, the Emperor, have failed to fulfill the Mandate of Heaven (Tianming), and, therefore, demands that you resign. Failure to comply with this demand, the group states, might result in harm to the hostages and destruction of the entire neighborhood.

You call a crisis meeting of your chief ministers. Among these advisors are Confucius, Laozi and Han Feizi. You tell each advisor that you want him to address the following questions: Who constitutes the Good Ruler? What is the criteria or standard the Good Ruler should use when making decisions? Finally, how can this standard be used to make a decision in this crisis? You will listen in turn to each minister's answers, and then decide which course of action to pursue.

Write an essay in which you indicate what answers each of the three advisors would give to the Emperor, and which position you, the Emperor, would adopt, and why.

Tips For Answering

This is a very complex essay question. In order to answer the question well it requires you to address a number of different problems. Perhaps one of the most important points to notice about this essay question is what it is not asking. It is not really asking you to decide what course of action each thinker would recommend in this crisis. Or rather, it is interested in using this simple question to raise a group of more sophisticated questions. It is these more complex questions that you are being asked to address. What are these questions?

The first of these questions is "Who is a Good Ruler?" What are the qualities or characteristics that define a leader or a ruler as being good or wise? Each of the three thinkers addresses this question in the works attributed to them. The answers they propose may agree on some points, but ultimately each thinker gives a very different description of the best type of ruler. What are the positions of each advisor and how do they differ?

What makes a ruler good or wise, it could be argued, is that he is able to act properly, and make the correct decisions for the good of his state. But this raises another question, what standard or criteria should a ruler employ in order to decide how to act? Is a good ruler one who preserves order in his country? Or is he one who the people respect and love? Or could it be that the good ruler is one who insures his own continued rule? Arriving at an answer to this question may in fact be necessary before one can define the Good Ruler.

There may be one more question even more deeply embedded in the essay assignment. It could be argued that for each of these Chinese thinkers their positions on the criteria that define good government are driven by their views on the nature of humans. Is man basically good or evil? Is it possible to make man better through education or religious practice, or will man always be untrustworthy? The answers that each thinker gave to these questions helped to determine what role, if any, he saw for government. In your essay, you might want to begin by examining each thinker's views on the nature of man.

Once you have addressed these questions in your essay it may be possible to say what specific advice each of these ancient Chinese thinkers might have given to the Emperor. Given the nature of man, and therefore the nature of good government, what specific action would be appropriate in this situation? And with which view of man, of government and of this crisis do you, the Emperor, agree? This is the decision that you need to make, but be sure to indicate what factors and reasons support your conclusions.

PART NINE PROJECTS FOR DEVELOPING RELIGIOUS EMPATHY

1. The Heart of the Dragon is an excellent documentary series on modern China produced by the British Broadcasting Corporation and shown a number of years ago on the Public Broadcasting Service here in America. Each episode of the series focuses on one aspect of Chinese culture, for example, marriage and the family, or the justice system. Two of the hour-long episodes deal specifically with various aspects of China's traditional teachings. If your college owns copies of this video you might want to see if you could borrow or arrange to view these episodes. You might also be able to find this video at a rental store that specializes in foreign and art videos.

   The segment called "Knowing" examines ancient Chinese science and technology, and its relation to China's recent attempts to modernize. Among the issues discussed is the role of Daoism and other alchemical and magical practices in ancient Chinese science. As you view this segment you might want to consider how ancient Chinese science was different from or similar to the science you might be studying at school. Would a scientist of today, do you think, accept what was being done as true "science"? Why? Also, you could consider what role Daoism and such ideas as yin-yang played in Chinese science? Is Daoism functioning here as a religion? As a science? As a philosophy? As a psuedo-science? If you would like to read more about science in ancient China, a work of truly impressive scholarship is Joseph Needham's multi-volume Science and Civilization in China.

   The other episode that deals with the religious traditions of China is the one titled "Believing". A portion of the episode examines the beliefs of modern China, and, in particular, the Chinese belief (or lack of belief) in what one of the speakers terms "Marxist-Leninist-Mao Zedong Socialist Thought". The central part of the hour, however, examines the traditional belief systems of China: folk religion, Buddhism, Daoism and Confucianism. This program raises a number of provocative issues you might want to consider. First, it makes the claim that much of the moral and social education shown in this episode is as Confucian as it is Maoist or Socialist. Is this true? Second, it claims that Confucianism should not be considered a religion, but rather a code of social behavior. Is this true? Can you figure out what definition of "religion" the program employs when it makes this judgment? Watch the program, examine some examples of how the Chinese live, and see if you agree with the conclusions of the program.

2. You might consider visiting a martial arts center or dôjô by yourself, or with a friend from the class. Many of the martial arts developed in China, Japan and Korea, and were influenced by various aspects of Confucianism, Daoism and Buddhism. You might be especially interested in observing the ancient Chinese practice of Taiji Chuan, which exhibits many of the ideas discussed in Daoism.

   If there is an instructor of Taiji in your area, ask him or her if you might visit a class and observe the students practicing their art. Explain that you are studying Chinese religion, and would be interested in seeing how some of these ideas may have influenced the martial arts. If you have this opportunity, pay attention to the nature of Taiji. What role does "balance" play in Taiji? Do you see any influences from the traditional teachings of China? Does the "form", the dance-like movement that is practiced every day, connect to any of the ideas or practices you have studied? Also observe, if you can, the more advanced students practicing "push-hands". What is the goal of such a practice? Would any of the Chinese thinkers be interested in such a practice? Why?

3. There are few gardens in the world as beautiful or serene as the best gardens of Japan. There are also few places where one can better observe the spirit of Shinto than in a Japanese-style garden. The Japanese-style garden has been influenced by many traditions over the centuries. Depending on the type and period of the Japanese garden, Zen or Pure Land Buddhism may also be an influence on a particular garden. However, Shinto has affected almost all styles of Japanese gardens. The very notion of setting aside an area for a garden is akin to the Shinto practice of marking off a Shinto shrine or a special tree or rock as the location of the kami.

   Many places in America now have a Japanese style garden that is open to the public. There are in Philadelphia, where this is being written, at least three Japanese gardens open to the public. If you have such a garden in your area, set aside some time for a visit. During your visit, first just observe the garden, and enjoy the views. Try to feel the mood that the garden creates. After a time, analyze more closely the specific elements that were combined to make the garden. What aspects of the garden seem different from a more Western style garden? Can you pick out any elements in the garden that may reflect a Shinto influence? What roles do rocks, trees and water play in the garden? Are any of these elements set aside in a special manner? If there are any buildings or man-made artifacts in the garden, what is their relation to the natural elements? Do they seem to contrast with the natural elements or harmonize with them? What type of order, if any, does the garden seem to project?

Those who can not visit a Japanese garden in person may want to learn about them by reading and examining pictures. Teiji Itoh has written a number of excellent books on the Japanese garden. Much the same questions can be asked as you look at the pictures in a good book on Japanese gardens.[4] But no book can ever substitute for the enjoyment of a visit to a peaceful garden on a beautiful Spring afternoon.

ANSWER KEY TO SELF-TEST SECTION

b) <u>Multiple Choice</u>

1. d	6. b
2. c	7. d
3. b	8. a
4. c	9. d
5. a	10. c

c) <u>True-False</u>

1. T	6. T
2. F	7. F
3. F	8. F
4. T	9. T
5. F	10. T

Notes

[1]Confucius, The Analects of Confucius, VII: 1-3, trans. Arthur Waley (New York: Vintage Books, 1938) 123

[2]Motoori Norinaga, Motoori Norinaga Zenshû, VI: 3-6, in Sources of Japanese Tradition, ed. Ryusaku Tsunoda et al., (New York: Columbia University Press, 1958) 520-521.

[3]Lao Tzu, Tao Te Ching, XIX, trans. D. C. Lau (New York: Penguin Books, 1963) 75.

[4]Teiji Itoh, The Japanese Garden, New Haven: Yale Press, 1972.

[4]Teiji Itoh, Space and Illusion in the Japanese Garden, New York: Weatherhill/Tankosha, 1973.

PART FOUR
Religions That Influenced East & West

PART ONE LEARNING OBJECTIVES

Doing these exercises, in conjunction with reading the textbook, should help you to achieve the following objectives. Read them and see how many you already have mastered; then study the following terms and concepts, and work through the exercises. After you have completed all the exercises, return to this section and review the objectives again.

You should be able to:

1. Identify the four major religions that have originated in India, and explain briefly when and how each tradition began.

2. Name at least three characteristics that most of these four traditions share.

PART TWO TERMS AND INDIVIDUALS

A) <u>Terms and Concepts</u>

Iraq

Tigris River

Euphrates River
Arabia
city-states
Farsi
Assyrians
Parsees
Mesopotamia
Egypt
Iran
Zoroastrianism
Medes

B) Individuals

Cyrus the Great

C) Individuals and Terms From Other Traditions

Aryans
Bible
Christianity
Islam
Judaism
Babylonian Talmud
Nestorianism

PART THREE GUIDED REVIEW

1. Ancient ____________ and ____________ were symbols to many peoples and cultures of advanced civilizations.

2. The country that today is called Iraq was known in the past as ____________________. The country that today is called Iran was known in the West as ________________.

3. At least two characteristics of the land and climate of Iraq are: ____________________ and ________________________.

4. In Mesopotamian city-states many rulers organized hierarchies of ____________.

5. At least two characteristics of the land and climate of Iran are: ____________________ and ________________________.

6. The major language spoken today in Iran is _____________.

7. One reason that Zoroastrianism may not have had a greater influence in the West is that ___________________________.

8. Three religious changes that occurred in the area of Iran and Iraq during the first millennium C.E. are that Jews ____________________________, Christians _____________ _____________, and Islam ____________________________.

PART FOUR QUESTIONS FOR CONSIDERATION

As you study the religions of Iraq and Iran, and read Part IV of the textbook, try to reflect upon, and even write out, responses to the following questions. These questions are designed to help you synthesize what you are learning about these two religions, and reach your own conclusions concerning the significance of these traditions.

1. The textbook claims that the religions of Iraq and Iran influenced both the East and the West. It also, however, states that these religions might have exerted a greater influence on the East and on the West. As you read the next chapter, try to consider what were the influences that religions from this area had on the East and the West? What historical, cultural or geographical factors might help account for these influences? What might have been some of the key factors limiting the influences of these religions?

2. After you have studied the religions of the Family of Abraham, try to compare the central characteristics of Babylonian religion and Zoroastrianism to those of religions in the Family of Abraham.

3. One characteristic that Judaism, Christianity and Islam are usually seen as sharing is the belief in One, righteous God who manifests Himself in human history. Would you say that such a belief is central to either ancient Babylonian religion or Zoroastrianism? Why have you reached this conclusion?

Chapter 7
The Ancient Religions of Iraq & Iran

CHAPTER SEVEN - THE ANCIENT RELIGIONS OF IRAQ AND IRAN

PART ONE LEARNING OBJECTIVES

Doing these exercises, in conjunction with reading the textbook, should help you to achieve the following objectives. Read them and see how many you already have mastered; then study the following terms and concepts, and work through the exercises. After you have completed all the exercises, return to this section and review the objectives again.

You should be able to:

1. Give a brief outline of the history of ancient Mesopotamia, and delineate some major differences between the geography, history and culture of Mesopotamia and Egypt.

2. Describe the nature and characteristics of Mesopotamian religion, including the major Mesopotamian myths and deities, some Mesopotamian religious practices and the views of the Absolute and of life and death.

3. Cite some examples of how Mesopotamian religion influenced and is related to the beliefs and practices of other traditions.

4. Give the life story of Zarathustra, illustrating how his

life exemplified Zoroastrian teachings.

5. Summarize the teachings of Zarathustra, especially addressing the question of whether his teachings reflect a monotheistic or a dualistic view of the Absolute.

6. Analyze the development of Zoroastrianism after the death of Zarathustra, focusing especially on the evolving understanding of the Absolute in Zoroastrianism.

7. Discuss and write about the Zoroastrian Worldview; in particular, the Zoroastrian view of the Absolute, the world, the human role, the fundamental problem and resolution for human beings, symbols and rituals, life after death, and relations with other religions.

8. Explain the significance of the fire sacrifice in Zoroastrianism.

PART TWO TERMS AND INDIVIDUALS

MESOPOTAMIA

A) Terms and Concepts

city-states
nations
ziggurats
cuneiform
Gilgamesh
Sumerian
Akkadian
Damuzi
Inanna
An
Enlil
Ninhursaga
Enki
Sin
Shamash
Ishtar
Tiamat
Apsu
Marduk
Ea
Tammuz
Ereshkigal
Nirgal
Kigal
Anunnaki
Enkidu
Huwawa
Utnapishtim

B) Individuals

Hammurabi
Nebuchadnezzar

C) Texts

Enuma Elish
The Epic of Gilgamesh

ZOROASTRIANISM

A) Terms and Concepts

Zoroastrianism
Ahura Mazda
Zoroastrians (Parsees)
daevas
ahuras
Spitama
Vohu Manah
Angra Mainyu
Amesha Spentas
Asha Vahista
Khshatra Vairya
Spenta Armaiti
Hourvatat
Ameretat
Chinvat Bridge
Magi
Sassanians
Manichaeism
Zurvanism
Zurvan
Anahita
Haoma
Fire Sacrifice
Soma
asha
Naozot
sudreh
kusti
dakhma
Sraosha
Uthamna ceremony
eschatology

B) Individuals

Zoroaster (Zarathustra)
Spitama
Dughdhova
Pourushaspa
King Vishtaspa
Cyrus the Great
Darius
Xerxes
Mani

C) Texts

Avesta
Gathas
Yasna
Visperad
Yashts
Videvdat

MESOPOTAMIA AND ZOROASTRIANISM

D) Individuals and Terms From Other Traditions

Egyptian
Persians
Romans
Greeks
Cyrus
Alexander the Great
Babylonian Talmud
Judaism

Christianity
Abraham
Veda (Rig-Veda)
Isaiah
Jesus Christ
people of the Book
Islam
Hinduism
Christian Trinity
Gospel According to Matthew
St. Augustine

PART THREE GUIDED REVIEW

1. The religions that developed in the countries that are now known as Iraq and Iran are identified in the textbook as _________________ religion, and as ________________________.

2. The structures similar to pyramids that were built in Mesopotamia are called ______________________.

3. The writing system used in Mesopotamia was _____________. This was done with ____.

4. After about 4000 B.C.E. the culture that dominated Mesopotamia was that of the ______________________________. The people who gained control around 2300 B.C.E. were called ______________________________.

5. In contrast to Egypt, events in Mesopotamia were often more ______________________________.

6. Jacobsen argues that the earliest Mesopotamian gods were perceived as __________________________________. In the third millennium, however, the gods were seen as __________. Finally, during the second millennium, gods were given roles as ____________________.

7. One of the best known deities was Ishtar, who was the goddess of ________________.

8. Two famous Babylonian epics are ____________________ and _________________________.

9. The Babylonian creation myth explains the creation of heaven, earth and man by the story of ____________________ ____ ____.

10. In the story that bears his name, the hero Gilgamesh journeys under the sea in search of _______________________.

While he is there, Utnapishtim tells him a story about ____________________.

11. One of the messages of the Gilgamesh story seems to be that man ____________________.

12. At the top of the ziggurat one would find ____________________.

13. In Mesopotamian religion humans interacted with the gods through rituals and symbols such as __________, __________, __________, and __________.

14. One of the most important contributions of the Mesopotamian worldview was the belief that human life should be lived ____________________.

15. Mesopotamian religion, unlike Egyptian religion, did not hold out the promise of ____________________.

16. Little is known about Iranian religion prior to Zoroastrianism because ____________________. It seems likely that it did involve worship of __________ and __________.

17. The founder of this movement that began in Persia was __________, who is also known by his Latin name of __________.

18. In Zoroastrianism there is a belief in __________, who is the Wise Lord and God. There is also, however, a belief in Angra Mainyu, who is ____________________.

19. Among the scriptures of Zoroastrianism is the __________, the book of the Law, and the __________, used to honor the lords.

20. The six intermediaries between God and human beings are the __________.

21. After death, a person's soul has to cross ____________________.

22. The ancient Zoroastrian priests who may appear in the account of Jesus's birth are the __________.

23. __________ developed from the teachings of Mani, who believed that the universe was ____________________.

24. Zoroaster combined the roles of __________ and
_____________.

25. The central act of communication for Zoroastrianism was
______________. The symbol for Ahura Mazda is
______________.

26. Among the symbols of Zoroastrianism the most important one is _________________. This is most likely to be found at the _____________________, which outsiders must not enter.

27. A major question in the Zoroastrian view of the Absolute is whether the good force and the evil force are
____.

28. The initiation rite into Zoroastrianism that occurs in the seventh year of a child's life is ___________________.

29. One of the most unusual aspects of Zoroastrianism is the ritual treatment of the dead. The body is usually taken to
______________________. At this place the body is
____.

30. One reason that the numbers of Zoroastrians may be in decline is that in general Zoroastrianism opposes ________
________________________.

PART FOUR ANALYZING TEXTS

Below are two texts that were not in the textbook. The texts, however, do contain ideas and concepts with which you should be familiar after reading the textbook and studying the selections in the textbook from primary religious documents. Read each text carefully, compare it to the primary documents you have studied and try to analyze each by answering the following questions: What are the main ideas in the text? What viewpoint or viewpoints might the author of the text represent? Is it possible to identify the specific thinker, discipline, movement, tradition or work from which the text derives? What intellectual, literary, social, cultural or historical influences are reflected in the text? For each of your conclusions, try to point to specific evidence in the text (e.g. terms, ideas, arguments, writing style, etc.) which supports your conclusion. Be careful that your conclusions do not exceed the evidence upon which they rest.

TEXT ONE

"O Maker of the material world, thou Holy One! Where are the rewards given? Where does the rewarding take place?" . . . Ahura Mazda answered: "When the man is dead, when his time is over, then the wicked, evil-doing Daevas cut off his eyesight. On the third night, when the dawn appears and brightens up, when Mithra, the god with beautiful weapons, reaches the all-happy mountains, and the sun is rising: then the fiend, named Vizaresha . . . carries off in bonds the souls of the wicked Daeva-worshipers who live in sin. The soul enters the way made by Time, and open both to the wicked and to the righteous. At the head of the Chinvad bridge, the holy bridge made by Mazda, they ask for their spirits and souls the reward for the worldly goods which they gave away here below. Then comes the beautiful, well-shapen, strong and well-formed maid, with the dogs at her sides . . . She makes the soul of the righteous one go up above the Haraberezaiti; above the Chinvad bridge she places it in the presence of the heavenly gods themselves. [1]

TEXT TWO

He who has seen everything, I will make known to the lands.
I will teach about him who experienced all things . . .
Anu granted him the totality of knowledge of all.
He saw the Secret, discovered the Hidden,
he brought information of (the time) before the Flood.
He went on a distant journey, pushing himself to exhaustion. [2]

PART FIVE SELF-TEST

A) Definitions and Descriptions - Write your own definition or description of each of the following terms, individuals or texts. After completing the self-test, check your answer with the definition or description given in the textbook.

1. dakhma ____
____
____.

2. the Fire Sacrifice ___________________________________
____
____.

3. cuneiform____
____
____.

4. city-states ____
____
____.

5. Manichaeism ____
____
____.

6. Ahura Mazda ____
____
____.

7. Gilgamesh ____
____
____.

8. eschatology ____
____
____.

9. Marduk ____
____
____.

10. Utnapishtim ____
____
____.

B) <u>Multiple Choice</u>

1. The story of Utnapishtim in the Mesopotamian <u>Epic of Gilgamesh</u> is a story of

a. The creation by the gods of an ideal person.
b. A great flood, and how a man, his family and the animals were saved in an ark.
c. A man who searches for immortality, but loses it to a serpent.
d. How man first discovered fire.

2. Which of the following religious traditions believed in the Fire Sacrifice?

a. Mesopotamian religion
b. Zoroastrianism
c. Egyptian religion
d. All of the above

3. For Zoroastrians the evil deity is

a. Ahura Mazda
b. Vohu Manah
c. Asha Vahista
d. Angra Mainyu

4. The earth mounds covered with bricks that were built in ancient Mesopotamia are called

a. ziggurats.
b. pyramids.
c. kofun.
d. Damuzi.

5. Which one of the following is not one of the six Amesha Spentas?

a. Ahura Mazda
b. Khshatra Vairya
c. Hourvatat
d. Asha Vahista

6. Which of these three religious thinkers or sources would be considered monotheistic?

a. Zarathustra
b. Mani
c. Zarathustra and Mani
d. <u>The Epic of Gilgamesh</u>

7. Which of the following deities is <u>not</u> one of the deities mentioned in the <u>Enuma Elish</u> creation story?

   a. Marduk
   b. Vishnu
   c. Tiamat
   d. Ea

8. What is the name of the only surviving Avesta?

   a. Veda
   b. Visperad
   c. Vinya
   d. Videvdat

9. What advice is Gilgamesh given concerning his search for immortal life?

   a. That he will find it through the Fire Sacrifice.
   b. That the gods have designed a way for men to become immortal.
   c. That he will find only death since this is what the gods have designed for man.
   d. That inner purity is the way to the immortal life.

10. The Sumerian period in Mesopotamia was during what time?

   a. about 4000 BCE - 2300 BCE
   b. about 3000 BCE - 2300 BCE
   c. about 2300 BCE - 539 BCE
   d. 539 BCE - 331 BCE

C) <u>True-False</u>

T F 1. The Mesopotamian epic entitled the <u>Enuma Elish</u> is a myth of creation.

T F 2. Zoroastrianism has both Fire Temples and Towers of Silence.

T F 3. Both Mesopotamian religion and Zoroastrianism can be termed religions of city-states.

T F 4. The Indians called the Zoroastrians Parsees, because they originally came from Persia.

T F 5. The writing system that the ancient Mesopotamians used is called hieroglyphics.

T F 6. The pattern of weather and flooding in Egypt was much more unpredictable than the pattern in Mesopotamia.

T F 7. The hymns of Zarathustra are collected in works called gathas.

T F 8. The Zoroastrian figure who believed in dualism was Zurvan.

T F 9. Eschatology means the doctrine of last things.

T F 10. The group known as the Magi who appear in the Gospel account of Jesus's birth were related to Zoroastrianism.

PART SIX ESSAY AND DISCUSSION QUESTIONS

1. Examine the question of whether Zarathustra espoused monotheism or dualism. How would you define each of these terms? Is a middle position between monotheism and dualism conceivable?

2. The Problem of Evil is a major issue in monotheistic religions: how could evil exist in a world created by an omnipotent, good God? How would Zoroastrianism explain the existence of evil in the world? Would Zoroastrianism have to address the Problem of Evil, and if so, how would it address it?

3. What is distinctive in the religious beliefs and practices of the ancient Mesopotamians?

4. Imagine that by some miracle of time travel you could actually live in ancient Mesopotamia of the second millennium. How did this society see man, his place in the universe and his relation to the gods? Would you want to live in a society which had this worldview? Why?

5. If you have already read the chapter on religions of ancient city-states consider how one can comparatively study the myths of two ancient cultures. Both the Mesopotamian myths and the Greek myths deal with the

actions of the gods and how these actions affect human life. To what extent, and in what specific ways, do the myths from the two traditions attempt to justify for humans the actions and ways of the gods? Are there any important differences in the myths of these two cultures?

PART SEVEN CONFRONTING QUESTIONS AND ISSUES

The two religions you have studied in this chapter have either ceased to exist, or are facing real struggles to survive as a tradition. This fact raises an interesting problem: what factors determine whether a religious tradition survives, or whether it disappears or is assimilated into rival traditions?

Imagine that you are writing a survival manual for religions in this difficult position. You will want to consider these two traditions, since both religions were in some ways very different, and yet both managed to influence much more dominant religions. How did both of these two traditions managed to develop, survive and even prosper? What historical factors contributed to the survival of each tradition? You might want to consider such factors as organizational structure, clan or tribe loyalty, initiation ceremonies, and political moves. What factors contributed to the decline of each tradition? Use your answers to these questions to outline a number of possible scenarios for the maximizing the survival of endangered religions.

PART EIGHT AN ESSAY QUESTION FOR DEEPER CONSIDERATION

Essay Question

The two religions discussed in this chapter have beliefs that raise interesting questions concerning the Problem of Evil. The Epic of Gilgamesh seems to suggest that mortality, and therefore suffering, is an inescapable fact of human existence. Zoroastrianism could be interpreted as either claiming that there are two radically different first principles in the Universe, one good and one evil, or claiming that there is a single, good, all-powerful deity who might in some way be temporarily limited by an evil presence. In an essay, examine the variety of ways in which The Epic of Gilgamesh and Zoroastrianism address the Problem of Evil.

Tips For Answering

You might want to begin the writing process by doing some brainstorming on, and researching what philosophers mean by, "The Problem of Evil" and "Theodicy". In very general terms The Problem of Evil can mean the attempt to understand and account for the apparent fact that there is a great deal of evil in the world, that too often bad things appear to happen to good people. Used in this sense, The Problem of Evil can refer to the attempts of Sakyamuni to come to terms with the issue raised by the Four Sights. Philosophers often use this term, however, in a more specific manner to refer to a philosophical problem that any potential monotheistic faith needs to address. In the narrow sense, The Problem of Evil can be stated something like this: "If there is an all-powerful, all-knowing and all-good Absolute in the Universe, then He/She must be able to eliminate evil, must know how to eliminate evil and must want to eliminate evil. However, evil exists. Therefore, such an Absolute must not exist." In what ways does The Problem of Evil, in either its narrow or general sense, constitute a problem in *The Epic of Gilgamesh*? In what way does it present a problem in the worldview of Zoroastrianism, and in particular in the thought of Zarathustra and Mani?

A "Theodicy" is any answer given by a believer to The Problem of Evil; that is to say, a theodicy attempts to explain how the existence of evil in the world is reconcilable with the existence of an Absolute. There are many different ways that theodicies attempt to reconcile the fact of evil and the existence of an Absolute. For example, some theodicies might question the authenticity or nature of evil. Others might propose a redefinition of what is meant by God, or all-powerful, or all-good. How does *The Epic of Gilgamesh* address the problem of evil? Could it be said to set-forth a theodicy? What theodicies do Zarathustra and Mani propose?

Since many philosophers have written on this problem and set-forth theodicies, you might also want to do some research in an encyclopedia or handbook of philosophy on the topics of "Evil", "The Problem of Evil" and "Theodicy". It might be interesting to contrast the approaches in these two traditions to the positions of St. Augustine, Christian Science, and the contemporary philosopher of religion, John Hick.

PART NINE PROJECTS FOR DEVELOPING RELIGIOUS EMPATHY

1. The Mesopotamian city-states described in this chapter of the textbook have ceased to exist. The art and the culture that they produced, however, still exists and continues to excite our imaginations. Some of the art from ancient Mesopotamia and Iran has been installed in museums throughout Europe and in America. It is through their art that many of us can most directly enter into the world of the Sumerians and Akkadians.

If you are in a city fortunate enough to have a collection of Mesopotamian art, take an afternoon to visit and view the collection. (If you do not have access to a collection of Mesopotamian art, you might want to examine pictures of this art in a history of world art in your library. Just bear in mind that a picture is only a faint reflection of the original.) Take your time to stroll the gallery, examine the objects and read the explanations concerning each object. Is some of the art familiar to you? Are any of the statues or paintings representations of gods or heroes discussed in this chapter? What seems to be the way in which humans are portrayed in the art? Is there a difference in the way men and women are portrayed? What does this tell us about Mesopotamian culture during this time?

2. A further project involving Mesopotamian and Greek art (or the art of any of the other city-states) requires some drawing. When you are in the museum, find an object that interests you and that is in some way related to the religions you have read about in this chapter. For example, you might be interested in a statue of the Greek god Zeus, or a carving of a Mesopotamian king receiving laws from a god. After you have selected an object, do the following: First, make a careful sketch of the object. When you are drawing the object, try to be aware of the proportions of the object and how it is constructed. Second, go to the library and try to read about objects of a similar nature. What is their place in the history of Greek or Mesopotamian art and civilization. Third, write down a brief response in which you consider how the object illuminates the culture that produced it, and how the two cultures differ as seen through their artifacts. If you find this helpful, you might get in the habit of keeping a combination sketch-note book for museum trips. Drawing an object often makes us more aware of the structure of the object, and the technique of the artist.

3. Every culture has a slightly different view of immortality. One of the best ways to study how a culture views death and the search for immortality is to examine how it treats its dead. Both Zoroastrianism and ancient Mesopotamian religion held very interesting beliefs concerning death, rituals for the dead, and life after death.

People in our society also have views concerning death, rituals for the dead, and life after death. For example, many people in our society take for granted the practice of burying the dead in cemeteries. However, the way in which we view cemeteries is a fairly recent phenomenon. The history of cemeteries is a fascinating subject. Go to a good reference encyclopedia and read the article on cemeteries. What were some of the different reasons for the popularity of cemeteries? How would you compare the Nineteenth century interest in cemeteries to our own view?

Then visit one of the older cemeteries in your town. Observe the graves from different historical periods. Can you notice differences in the style of the tombstones? Can you pinpoint the different styles, and the rough time periods when each style was in vogue? What do the various styles of tombstones (or crypts) and the messages on the tombstones tell us about the view of death and the search for immortality during each period? What do the most recent tombstones tell you about our view of death today?

ANSWER KEY TO SELF-TEST

B) Multiple Choice

1. b	6. a
2. b	7. b
3. d	8. d
4. a	9. c
5. a	10. a

C) True-False

1. T	6. F
2. T	7. T
3. F	8. F
4. T	9. T
5. F	10. T

Notes

[1]Selection from "Zendavesta," The Portable World Bible, ed. Robert O. Ballou (1944; New York: Penguin Books, 1985) 190-191.

[2]Maureen Gallery Kovacs (trans.), The Epic of Gilgamesh (Stanford, CA: Stanford University Press, 1985) 3.

PART FIVE
Religions of the Family of Abraham

PART ONE LEARNING OBJECTIVES

Doing these exercises, in conjunction with reading the textbook, should help you to achieve the following objectives. Read them and see how many you already have mastered; then study the following terms and concepts, and work through the exercises. After you have completed all the exercises, return to this section and review the objectives again.

You should be able to:

1. Identify the three major religions that comprise the "family of Abraham", and explain briefly when and how each tradition began.

2. Name at least three characteristics that these three traditions share.

PART TWO TERMS AND INDIVIDUALS

A) Terms and Concepts

Judaism

Christianity

Islam
Torah
Promised Land
covenant
New Testament
Bible
Mount Sinai
Israel
High Priest

B) <u>Individuals</u>

Abraham
Jacob
Moses
Ishmael
Isaac
Jesus of Nazareth
Muhammad

PART THREE GUIDED REVIEW

1. One statement that members of the Jewish, Christian and Islamic religious traditions could all affirm is ______________________________.

2. Another similarity between the three religions in this "family" is that they all trace their beginnings back, in some way, to __________________.

3. Judaism keeps faith with the covenant as it is expressed in the ______________.

4. The three patriarchs, or founding figures, that Judaism sees at the beginning of its history are _____________, ___________________, and ____________________.

5. Christianity grew out of the teaching of _________________.

6. Although Christians see themselves as having a heritage that goes back to Abraham, they also believe there is a ___________________ with God.

7. Islam traces itself back to Abraham through ___________ who was __________________.

8. Although Islam does not reject the message of Jews and Christians, it does believe that ________________ entered into the messages.

9. Islam believes that the teaching as received by Muhammad was ______________________________.

PART FOUR QUESTIONS FOR CONSIDERATION

As you study the religions of the family of Abraham and read Part V of the textbook try to reflect upon, and even write out, responses to the following questions. These questions are designed to help you synthesize what you are learning about these religions, and reach your own conclusions concerning the significance of these traditions.

1. The textbook groups all these three religions under the term "Religions of the Family of Abraham." What does the concept of a "family" mean? Can you think of different definitions of "family?" How would each of these ideas of family apply to these three traditions? How well does the concept of "family" fit, and what might be some problems with using this concept to understand these three traditions?

2. If you have already studied the religions of India, compare the view of the Absolute in Judaism, Christianity and Islam to the view of the Absolute in Hinduism. How would you characterize how each group of traditions views the Absolute? Even though Hinduism does not trace its heritage back to Abraham, what are the similarities between how these three religions look at the Absolute and how Hinduism sees the Absolute? Are there important differences?

One characteristic that Judaism, Christianity and Islam are usually seen as sharing is the belief in one, righteous God who manifests Himself in human history. Would you say that such a belief is central to Hinduism, or some part of Hinduism? Why have you reached this conclusion?

3. Many of the religions that you have read tell creation stories. The three religions of Family of Abraham also contain stories of creation. Make a chart of all the creation stories you have read, listing the characteristics of each story. What does each story show us about the nature of the religious tradition that uses it?

Chapter 8
Judaism

PART ONE LEARNING OBJECTIVES

Doing these exercises, in conjunction with reading the textbook, should help you to achieve the following objectives. Read them and see how many you already have mastered; then study the following terms and concepts, and work through the exercises. After you have completed all the exercises, return to this section and review the objectives again.

You should be able to:

1. Analyze the nature of Torah and discuss its significance and role in Judaism.

2. Examine the concept of a "revealed-historical religion", how Judaism is a revealed-historical religion, and how this contrasts with the religions studied earlier.

3. Outline the stories of Abraham's covenant with God, and the Exodus from Egypt, and analyze the importance of "covenant" in the history of the Jewish people.

4. Describe the nature and characteristics of the Prophetic Movement, including at least two pre-exilic prophets and their messages.

5. Explain how modern "critical" scholarship believes the

Pentateuch was edited, and the significance of these discoveries.

6. Analyze the development of Judaism from the post-exilic prophets to the beginning of the Roman administration of Palestine, including a discussion of the beginning of congregational worship, the Greek influence on Judaism, and the nature of Wisdom literature.

7. Describe Judaism during the Roman administration of Palestine, including the Messianic movements, Jewish revolts against Roman rule and the birth of Rabbinic Judaism.

8. Define what is meant by Talmudic Judaism, explain the process by which the Talmud was compiled and discuss the centrality of Talmud for Jewish life.

9. Offer an overall description of Medieval Judaism, illustrating this by reference to at least two Medieval philosophers and Medieval Jewish mysticism.

10. Describe the changes Judaism went through during the Modern Age, including the influence of the Enlightenment on Jewish thinkers and the birth of the Reform, the movements of Modernism and Jewish feminism, and the Conservative and Reconstructionist movements.

11. Recognize and discuss the importance of the Holocaust and the State of Israel for Judaism in the Twentieth Century.

12. Discuss and write about the Worldview of Judaism, in particular, the views of Judaism on the Absolute, the world, the human role, the fundamental problem and resolution for human beings, community and ethics, symbols and rituals, and life after death.

13. Explain the concept of <u>kashruth</u>, and discuss how diet and food can be an expression of a religious commitment.

14. Examine alternative answers to the problem of "Who is a Jew", and why this problem has been so controversial.

PART TWO TERMS AND INDIVIDUALS

A) Terms and Concepts

monotheism
Judaism
"conservative"
"critical"
history
covenant
Passover
Mount Sinai
theocracy
"Ehyeh-Asher-Ehyeh"
Canaan
Baal
seer
Hebrews
prophets
the First Temple
Yahweh
"J"
"D"
synagogue
Judea
theodicy
Seleucids of Syria
Sabbath
Maccabean revolt
Sadducees
Essenes
Qumran community
Sanhedrin
diaspora
Halakhah
the Second Temple
kosher
Karaites
Kabbalah
ghetto
Modernism
Reform Judaism
Orthodox Judaism
Columbus Platform
mitzvot
kippot/yamulkes
Hasidism
Balfour Declaration

Western Wall (Wailing Wall)
Jerusalem
"traditional"
"liberal"
heilsgeschichte
sacrifice
matzah
Ark of the Covenant
Shema
Canaanites
The Judges
Asherah
Levites
Samaria
Assyrians
Babylonian Exile
Elohim
"E"
"P"
rabbi

scribe
Hellenism
circumcision
Hanukkah
Zealots
Pharisees
Messiah
Rabbinic Judaism
Aggadah
allegorical method
Masada
"king's serfs"
Geonim
En Soph
the Inquisition
Mensch
Pittsburgh Platform
Conservative Judaism
Zionism
kashruth (kashrut)
Reconstructionism
Zaddik
Holocaust

kibbutzim
Adonai
Jewish feminism
shohet
halakhah
written law
shofar
Yom Kippur
Purim
Shavuot
Seder
Bat Mitzvah

Arab-Israeli Conflict
sheol
shehitah
Haggadah
aggadah
oral law
Rosh Hashana
Hanukkah
Passover

Bar Mitzvah

B) Individuals

Abraham (Abram)
Lot
Hagar
Jacob (Israel)
Moses
Samuel
David
Rehoboam
Queen Jezebel
Nathan
Hosea
Micah
Ezra
Jeremiah
Nehemiah
Simon
Pompey
Pilate
Florus
Titus
Flavius Silva
Rabbi Akiba
Hadrian
Rabbi Meir
Saadia ben Joseph
Judah Halevi
Moses de Leon
King Ferdinand
Baruch Spinoza
Abraham Geiger
Samson Raphael Hirsch
Isaac Mayer Wise
Mordecai Kaplan
Elie Wiesel

Sarah
Isaac
Ishmael
Joseph
Joshua
Saul
Solomon
Elijah
Bathsheba
Amos
Isaiah
Nebuchadnezzar
Ezekiel
Second Isaiah (Deutro-Isaiah)
Mattathias
Judas (son of Mattathias)
Judas the Galilean
Philo Judaeus
Vespasian
Flavius Josephus
Yohanan ben Zakkai
Bar Kokhba
Rabbi Hillel
Rabbi Judah
Anan ben David
Moses ben Maimon (Maimonides)
Isaac Luria
Queen Isabella
Moses Mendelssohn
Zacharias Frankel
David Einhorn
Solomon Schecter
Israel Baal Shem
Martin Buber

Hermann Cohen
Chaim Weizmann
Theodore Herzl
Emil Fackenheim
David Ben-Gurion
Leo Baeck
Captain Alfred Dreyfus
Anne Frank
Elie Wiesel
Marc Ellis
Golda Meir

C) Texts

The Jewish Bible (Tanakh)
Genesis
Leviticus
Deuteronomy
Joshua
First and Second Samuel
Isaiah
Ezekiel
Joel
Obadiah
Micah
Habakkuk
Haggai
Malachi
Psalms
Job
Ruth
Ecclesiastes
Daniel
Nehemiah
Septuagint
Mishnah
Gemarah
Aggadah
Midrash
Mishneh Torah
Guide for the Perplexed
Siddur
Nathan the Wise
The Jewish State
Judaism and Christianity
Exodus
Numbers
The Prophets (Nevi'im)
Judges
First and Second Kings
Jeremiah
Hosea
Amos
Jonah
Nahum
Zephaniah
Zechariah
The Writings (Kethuvim)
Proverbs
Song of Songs
Lamentations
Esther
Ezra
First and Second Chronicles
Wisdom literature
Talmud
Babylonian Talmud
Halakhah
The Kuzari
Shirei Ziyyon (Poems of Zion)
Yigdal
Zohar
I and Thou
The Idea of the Holy

D) Individuals and Terms From Other Traditions

Pharaoh Ramses II
Islam
Muslim
Muhammad
Horus
Christianity
muezzin
Dome of the Rock
Isis
Marduk

Babylonians	Cyrus of Persia
Alexander the Great	Aristotle
John the Baptist	Jesus of Nazareth
King Herod	Rome
Clement	Origen
John Locke	Rene Descartes
Gotthold Ephraim Lessing	Rudolph Otto

PART THREE GUIDED REVIEW

1. Judaism is a religion which grew out ________________.

2. The three main headings of the Jewish Bible are ______________, ____________________ and ____________________.

3. A conservative approach to interpreting the Bible could be defined as ____.
A critical approach to interpreting the Bible could be defined as ____.

4. The concept of <u>heilsgeschichte</u> used by Biblical scholars means ____.

5. One of the main acts of worship in Judaism from the time of Abraham until the destruction of the Second Temple was ______________________.

6. The idea of a covenant is a ____________________________.

7. The Jewish holiday of Passover commemorates ____________ ____.

8. The unleavened bread that is eaten during Passover symbolizes ____.

9. The wooden chest containing the tablets with the Ten Commandments was called ________________________________.

10.The <u>Shema</u> is ____________________________________.
The line from the <u>Shema</u> that comes from Deuteronomy 6:4 reads ____.

11.The religion of the Canaanites consisted of ____________ ____.

12. Prophets in Judaism were those who __________________ ____.

13. The image that Hosea used in his teachings was that of Israel as ______________________________.

14. When the First Temple was destroyed, many of the Jews who were living in Judah were exiled to ______________________.

15. According to most Biblical scholars the first five books are edited documents that contain the writings of _________ sources.

16. Scholars label these writers as ____ , ___ , ____ and _____. The work of Deuteronomy is credited to _____.

17. The difference between the Temple and the synagogue worship was that worship in the Temple centered around ______________________, while congregational worship centered around _________________________.

18. The rabbi differs from a priest in the Temple in that ____.

19. Scholars believe that chapters forty through sixty-six in the book of the Bible termed <u>Isaiah</u> were written by _________ ______________________ at the time of __________________ __________________________.

20. The influential Greek translation of Hebrew scriptures is the ________________________.

21. Wisdom literature is defined as _______________________ ____.

22. The Maccabees were ___________________________________. It was during their struggle that the events occurred that are the basis for the Jewish holiday of ___________________.

23. The Pharisees were __________________________________ ____.

24. During the time of Roman rule of Palestine the Jewish party that believed in a forceful overthrow of Roman rule was the ______________________.

25. The highest Jewish court and governing Jewish body before the destruction of the Second Temple was _________________.

26. The incident that sparked the Jewish rebellion against the Romans was ____.

27. The canon of the Jewish Bible was assembled by ____________ C.E.

28. The Babylonian Talmud is a combination of the ____________ and the ____________. The nature of the Talmud is ____________.

29. Saadia ben Joseph is famous for combining ____________ ____________.

30. The Thirteen Articles of Maimonides includes as essential beliefs of Judaism (list three) ____________, ____________, and ____________.

31. According to the Zohar the world that we experience through our senses is ____________ ____________. At the top of a hierarchy of male-female dualities is ____________.

32. During the Medieval Period many Jews made a living by lending money because ____________ and because ____________.

33. Under Ferdinand and Isabella the Jews living in Spain had to choose between ____________ and ____________.

34. Spinoza was excommunicated by the rabbis because he taught such ideas as ____________.

35. The teachings of Moses Mendelssohn took the position that people of different religions ____________.

36. The four main branches of Judaism in the United States are ____________, ____________, ____________ and ____________.

37. In regard to keeping Kosher, Reform Judaism ____________ ____________.

38. Mordecai Kaplan founded the school known as ____________ which emphasizes ____________.

39. The term Hasidim means ____________.

40. Today, the term "The Holocaust" refers to ____________ ____________.

41. The cooperative farms that have played a major role in building the State of Israel are called _______________.

42. Judaism has usually expressed the nature of God in the analogy of a _____________________.

43. Judaism's view of the nature of the world and the body is ____.

44. Mitzvot could be defined as _______________________.

45. Examples that Jewish feminists are pushing for include _________________________ and _______________________.

46. Robert Gordis argues that there is, and should be, a tension in Judaism between ________________________ and ___________________________.

47. Arthur Hertzberg states that traditional writings in Judaism have produced two reasons for kashruth: _________________________ and _____________________.

48. The Halakhic answer to the question of "Who is a Jew?" is ____.

PART FOUR ANALYZING TEXTS

Below are three texts that were not in the textbook. The texts, however, do contain ideas and concepts with which you should be familiar after reading the textbook and studying the selections in the textbook from primary religious documents. Read each text carefully, compare it to the primary documents you have studied and try to analyze each by answering the following questions: What are the main ideas in the text? What viewpoint or viewpoints might the author of the text represent? Is it possible to identify the specific thinker, discipline, movement, tradition or work from which the text derives? What intellectual, literary, social, cultural or historical influences are reflected in the text? For each of your conclusions, try to point to specific evidence in the text (e.g. terms, ideas, arguments, writing style, etc.) which supports your conclusion. Be careful that your conclusions do not exceed the evidence upon which they rest.

TEXT ONE

When she pursues her lovers she will not overtake them,
when she looks for them she will not find them;
then she will say,
'I will go back to my husband again;
I was better off with him than I am now.'
For she does not know that it is I who gave her
corn, new wine, and oil,
I who lavished upon her silver and gold
which they spent on the Baal.
Therefore I will take her back
my corn at the harvest and my new wine at the vintage,
and I will take away the wool and the flax
which I gave her to cover her naked body;
so I will show her up for the lewd thing she is . . .

I will punish her for the holy days
when she burnt sacrifices to the Baalim.[1]

TEXT TWO

MISHNAH. Every kind of flesh is forbidden to be cooked in milk, excepting the flesh of fish and of locusts; and it is also forbidden to place upon the table [flesh] with cheese, excepting the flesh of fish and of locusts. If a person vowed to abstain from flesh, he may partake of the flesh of fish and of locusts.

GEMARA. It follows [from our Mishnah] that the flesh of fowls is prohibited by the law of Torah; now in accordance with whose view would this be? It surely is not in accordance with R. Akiba's view, for R. Akiba maintains that the flesh of wild animals and of fowls is not prohibited by the law of Torah. Consider now the final clause,"if a person vowed to abstain from flesh, he may partake of the flesh of fish and locusts." It follows however that he is forbidden the flesh of fowl, which is in accordance with R. Akiba's view, namely, that any variation concerning which the agent would ask for special instructions is deemed to be of the same species. . . R. Joseph said, The author [of our Mishnah] is Rabbi [Judah the Prince] who incorporated the views of various Tannaim: with regard to vows he adopted the view of R. Akiba, and with regard to flesh [cooked] in milk he adopted the view of the Rabbis.[2]

TEXT THREE

> We recognize in the Bible the record of the consecration of the Jewish people to its mission as the priest of the one God, and value it as the most potent instrument of religious and moral instruction. . . We recognize in the Mosaic legislation a system of training the Jewish people for its mission during it national life in Palestine, and today we accept as binding only its moral laws, and maintain only such ceremonies as elevate and sanctify our lives, but reject all such as are not adapted to the view and habits of modern civilization. [3]

PART FIVE SELF-TEST

A) Definitions and Descriptions - Write your own definition or description of each of the following terms, individuals or texts. After completing the self-test, check your answer with the definition or description given in the textbook.

1. mitzvot ____
____
____.

2. Haggadah ____
____
____.

3. Pharisees ____
____
____.

4. halakhah ____
____
____.

5. synagogue ____
____
____.

6. Shema ____
____
____.

7. "J" ____
____
____.

8. rabbi ____
____
____.

9. Passover ____
____
____.

10. Gemarah ____
____
____.

B) Multiple Choice

1. The branch of Judaism in America that attempts to moderate between the rejection of all rituals and mitzvot, and a very strict observation of all traditional obligations is

   a. Conservative Judaism.
   b. Orthodox Judaism.
   c. Reform Judaism.
   d. Reconstructionist Judaism.

2. Which of the following is not one of the three divisions of the Hebrew Bible?

   a. Torah
   b. Wisdom
   c. Prophets
   d. Writings

3. The Greek translation of the Hebrew Bible was the

   a. Vulgate.
   b. Tanakh.
   c. Septuagint.
   d. Wisdom literature.

4. Which one of the following is not used to denote an author of material in the first five books of the Bible?

   a. "J"
   b. "T"
   c. "P"
   d. "E"

5. The juristic tradition, or legal material from the Torah, is called

   a. Midrash
   b. Talmud
   c. Aggadah
   d. Halakhah

6. Which of the following was <u>not</u> one of the Jewish sects at the time of Jesus of Nazareth?

   a. Essenes
   b. Sanhedrin
   c. Zealots
   d. Sadducees

7. Which Jewish holiday commemorates the Exodus from Egypt?

   a. Yom Kippur
   b. Rosh Hashana
   c. Purim
   d. Passover

8. The teachers who called Israel back to a pure religion, and also criticized the reliance on sacrificial rites were called

   a. Priests.
   b. Rabbis
   c. Prophets.
   d. Sages.

9. It could be said that Judaism begins with whose encounter with God?

   a. Moses
   b. Joseph
   c. David
   d. Abraham

10. The Medieval Jewish thinker who formulated 13 articles that all Jews should agree upon was

   a. Moses Mendelssohn.
   b. Judah Halevi.
   c. Maimonides.
   d. Saadia ben Joseph.

C) True-False

T F 1. Bar Kokhba was held to be the Messiah by the famous Rabbi Akiba.

T F 2. Most critical scholars believe that the Torah was written by Moses.

T F 3. The Babylonian Talmud is a combination of the Mishnah and the Gemarah.

T F 4. The Zohar believed that this world is the highest reality.

T F 5. Spinoza believed that the Old Testament taught an idea of immortality.

T F 6. Recontructionism rejects any supernatural elements in Judaism.

T F 7. The position of the Conservative Movement was set out in the Pittsburgh Platform.

T F 8. Judaism could be classified as a revealed-historic religion.

T F 9. A scribe was the person who wrote down the teachings of the prophets as they spoke.

T F 10. The book called "Isaiah" contains the writings of at least two different prophets.

PART SIX ESSAY AND DISCUSSION QUESTIONS

1. Examine the role of Torah in Jewish history. In what ways would it be accurate to claim that Judaism is the way of Torah? Give examples of how different Jewish figures and movements have interpreted Torah.

2. Explain how the first five books of the Jewish Bible were written and edited.

3. What does the term "covenant" mean, and how could the history of the Jewish people be understood as an ongoing covenant between God and his people?

4. Using two pre-exilic prophets, describe the Prophetic movement, and examine in what ways it was a challenge to the Temple-centered religion?

5. What were some of the basic differences between the Judaism of the time of Jesus and the Second Temple, and the Rabbinic Judaism that evolved after the destruction of the temple?

6. What was the Talmud and what role did it play in Medieval Judaism? What does the author mean when he says "Medieval Judaism was Talmudic Judaism?"

7. What is "mysticism" in general? What is distinctive about Jewish mysticism?

8. What role does Israel play in modern Judaism? What challenges face Israel in the future?

PART SEVEN CONFRONTING ISSUES AND ANSWERS

The author of the textbook mentions a number of issues that confront modern day Judaism. Near the top of any such list for almost all Jews in America is the question of Israel. American Jews have loyally and strongly supported Israel throughout her existence, and they continue to do so today. Given the horror of the Holocaust and the tenuous position of Jews in so much of the world, American Jews believe that the existence of the State of Israel is vital for all Jews. While almost all Jews support the existence of a Jewish state, however, this does not mean that there is not a debate over what should be the nature of such a state. For many Jews, Israel is not just a physical location or a political entity, it is also a symbol. The question for many Israelis, American Jews and friends of Israel is how to define the symbolic nature of Israel.

Consider and reflect on the following questions: What does the establishment of the state of Israel mean in conjunction with the Holocaust? Does the existence of Israel serve as a sign of hope in the face of such utter evil? Should Israel be a model for other nations, and if so, does this mean that Israel should be held to higher standards than her neighbors? What role, if any, should the belief in an eternal covenant between God and the descendants of Abraham have in answering this question? Can Israel afford to be held to higher standards than other countries? Can she afford not to be held to higher standards? Is Israel primarily a political entity, or is it also a spiritual and a moral entity? If Israel is primarily a Jewish state, what does that mean? Does it mean that non-Jews in the country are not full citizens? If you are Jewish, you have probably thought about these questions a great deal. If you are not Jewish, you might want to talk about them with a close Jewish friend. Listen carefully to understand how your friend feels about these issues, and how they influence his or her life.

PART EIGHT AN ESSAY FOR DEEPER CONSIDERATION

Essay Question

Ludwig Lewisohn raises the question in this manner: "What is a Jew? What is it to be a Jew? Are Jews a religious community, like the Roman or Greek Churches? Or are Jews an ethnic group, like the Negroes? Or are they a secular community, formed by historic forces, which is a vague enough term, like the Danes or the Dutch?"[4] Another, less existentialist, way of phrasing this query is, what is normative Judaism? What are the criteria, if any, that determine if an individual remains within the bounds of Judaism?

Examine this question in light of your study of Judaism. Illustrate your points with specific references to the thinkers, ideas or movements you have studied.

Tips For Answering

One of the major points you should discuss in your essay is the proposed answers that Lewisohn mentions in the quote. He suggests three alternative answers: Judaism as a religious community, as an ethnic group and as a secular community. Using Lewisohn's alternatives you could approach the problem in the following fashion:

a) You first could clarify the meaning of each of these terms. What does each of these terms mean? Are the examples he gives clarifying or confusing? Can you think of any other alternatives?

b) After you have clarified the three choices you could examine the evidence from Jewish history and belief. Does either of these three choices explain how Jews have identified themselves, and drawn the bounds of the community? Are the criteria for being Jewish religious, social or ethnic criteria?

c) If none of these three options explains what being Jewish means, could some combination of the three be more accurate? Lewisohn does not consider this alternative, and it may be the case that Judaism is a combination of the three aspects.

d) Your essay could also consider a more radical answer. Perhaps what makes one Jewish is something like a relationship to history, or a commitment to a covenant. Indeed, this is the general approach that Lewisohn takes later in his article. You should consider the possibility that Judaism functions in a unique way among world religions.

PART NINE PROJECTS FOR DEVELOPING RELIGIOUS EMPATHY

1. Since the destruction of the Second Temple one of the centers of Judaism has been the synagogue. A synagogue is a place for prayer and a place to read and study Torah. Many synagogues welcome visits by a person trying to better understand Judaism.

   If you have a Jewish friend who belongs to a congregation ask if you might visit a service with him or her. You might want your friend to explain beforehand what will occur during the service, and what are the different aspects of the service. It might also be helpful and polite to meet the rabbi beforehand, and explain why you will be attending. He or she would probably be glad to answer any questions that you might have.

   During the Sabbath service observe the congregation, how are they acting? Do they seem to be focused on the rabbi, or are they interacting among themselves? What is the inter-personal dynamic? How is the inside of the synagogue structured? Where is the center of attention? Does there seem to be a hierarchical arrangement of space? Are any special items of clothing being worn by the people and the rabbi, and if so, what do they signify? Is music part of the ritual? If it is, how would you describe the music? Are there any artistic representations inside the synagogue? If so, where are they, and what is their nature? How might what you see be different if you were in a Reform (or Conservative, or Orthodox) congregation? What does the Jewish ritual and worship you see here indicate about the nature of Jewish faith and belief?

2. The horror of the Holocaust, during which at least six million Jews were killed, is an event that no one can fully understand, and yet an event people should never forget. A number of excellent documentary films have been made on the Holocaust, but one of the best is the black and white film Night and Fog. Many colleges have copies of the film, as do the better video stores. Try to get a copy and watch it. It is not a movie designed to make you feel good, but it will raise questions that can not be ignored.

   Among the questions you should ponder as you watch the film are: Where was God when such a thing happened? Could there be a God if there is so much evil in the world? Which was more evil, committing such acts, or not protesting the commission of such acts? What is the meaning of the Jews as a chosen people? Is the image that Second Isaiah uses of a suffering servant applicable here, or does this level of brutality render that concept meaningless, or worse? Is the message of the Holocaust that Jews must rely on themselves to survive, not trusting in other nations?

   After you have seen the film, you might also want to read two excellent books by the novelist Elie Wiesel, Night and The Town Beyond the Wall. These novels raise many of these same issues.

ANSWER KEY TO SELF-TEST

B) Multiple Choice

1. a	6. b
2. b	7. d
3. c	8. c
4. b	9. d
5. d	10. c

C) True-False

1. T	6. T
2. F	7. F
3. T	8. T
4. F	9. F
5. F	10. T

Notes

[1] Hosea II:7-13, *The New English Bible* (Oxford, Oxford University Press, 1970).

[2] Mishnah VIII.1, Gemara page 104a, *The Babylonian Talmud*, ed. I. Epstein, Part I, Vol.4 (London: The Soncino Press, 1948) 576.

[3] "The Pittsburgh Platform" Article 2, 3, *Basic Sources of the Judaeo-Christian Tradition*, Fred Berthold, et al. (Engelwood Cliffs, N.J.: Prentice-Hall, Inc., 1962) 350.

[4] Ludwig Lewisohn, *What is This Jewish Heritage?* (New York: Bnai Brith Hillel Foundations, 1954) 1.

Chapter 9
Christianity

PART ONE LEARNING OBJECTIVES

Doing these exercises, in conjunction with reading the textbook, should help you to achieve the following objectives. Read them and see how many you already have mastered; then study the following terms and concepts, and work through the exercises. After you have completed all the exercises, return to this section and review the objectives again.

1. Relate the life story of Jesus of Nazareth, discussing how events in his life exemplifies Christian teachings and the significance for Christians of Jesus's life, death and resurrection.

2. Write about and analyze the teachings of Jesus as they are contained in the Gospel accounts, addressing the issue of how Jesus's teaching compared and contrasted with that of the Judaism of his day.

3. Explain why the significance of the Resurrection for Christians, and describe how Paul interpreted the meaning of the Resurrection and the Christian message.

4. Examine the issue of "Christology" (the study of <u>who</u> Jesus was and who his followers thought he was), exploring how Jesus referred to himself and saw himself, and how the

early Jesus movement and the early Church attempted to understand Jesus's nature and role.

5. Discuss the development of the early Church, including how the Church addressed the question of the relation between the new Church and Judaism.

6. Name the main groups of scriptures in the New Testament, and explain the process by which the four Gospel accounts were written and compiled.

7. Explain the major doctrinal and organizational developments in Christianity from the time of Clement until the division between the Roman and Orthodox Churches. You should be able to discuss, in particular, the role of Greek philosophy in the formation of doctrine, the major heresies the Church addressed, the councils at Nicea and Chalcedon, and the significance of monasticism.

8. Give a description of the theology of Thomas Aquinas, examine the role reason plays in his thought, and detail at least one of his arguments for the existence of God.

9. Analyze the role and significance of the Reformation movement, describe the major distinctions between the three major streams of this movement and name the major points of contention between the Protestant reformers and the Roman Catholic Church.

10. Describe the development of Christianity from the time of the Reformation until the present day. You should be able to discuss and illustrate the nature of Christian missionary endeavors, the role of Christianity among Afro-Americans, and liberation theology.

11. Discuss and write about the Christian Worldview; in particular, the Christian view of The Absolute, the world, humans, the fundamental problem and resolution for human beings, community and ethics, rituals and symbols, life after death, and other religious traditions.

12. Discuss the concept of "authority" in Christianity, the four foundations of authority, why this is a source of division in Christianity and how scholars have attempted to analyze this issue.

PART TWO TERMS AND INDIVIDUALS

A) Terms and Concepts

Christ
Messiah
hermeneutics
Holy Spirit
miracle
Pharisees
rabbi
Prodigal Son
Palm Sunday
Gethsemane
Zealots
resurrection
apostle
church
Paul (Saul) of Taurus
mystery religions
Judaizers
gospel
Roman Catholicism
catechumen
Q (Quelle)
apocalyptic literature
psalms
bishops
presbyters
Coptic church
Ethiopian Christianity

homoousia
Council of Nicaea
heresy
Monophysites
Trinity
economia
allegorical method
St. Benedict's Rule
Dominicans
autocephalic
Pope (Bishop of Rome)
iconostasis
iconodule
scholasticism
The Crusades
Protestant
theology

Son of God
incarnation
Kingdom of God
Satan
Samaritan
Mosaic Law
parables

Holy Communion/Last Supper
Son of Man
Golgotha
Pentecost
kerygma
speaking in tongues
pantheon
Gentile question
agape
Rome
apocalypse
canon
epistles
Nag Hammadi
sacraments
elders
heretics
Nestorian Christianity
Logos
ecumenical
Arians
Nicene Creed
Adoptionist
Council of Chalcedon
persona
filoque
stigmata
Franciscan
deacons
patriarch of Constantinople
excommunicate
iconoclast
patriarchates
Thomism
synod
Reformation
Ninety-Five Theses

indulgence
St. Peter's Basilica
Peace of Augsburg
Council of Trent
Baptism
Confirmation
Marriage
Holy Orders
Penance
Anointing of the Sick
humanism
Presbyterian
Anabaptists
Lutheran
Church of England (Anglicans)
Society of Friends (Quakers)
The Catholic Reformation
Society of Jesus (Jesuits)
"hidden Christians"
Puritans
Separatists
Baptists
Methodist
Great Awakening
Eastern Orthodox Church
separation of church and state
Deism
Theism
Civil Religion
Church of Christ, Scientist
World Council of Churches
National Council of Churches
Unification Church
Divine Principle
Church of Jesus Christ of Latter-day Saints
First Vatican Council
Second Vatican Council
liberation theology
the Incarnation
Resurrection of the Dead
Atonement
mystery
theodicy
tithing
The Mass
Maundy Thursday
Good Friday
Christmas
Easter
Hell
Heaven
anno Domini
authority

B) Individuals

Jesus of Nazareth
John the Baptist
Zechariah
King Herod
Peter
Mary
Joseph
Elijah
Judas
Pilate
Barabbas
Joseph of Arimathea
St. Augustine
Paul (Saul of Taurus)
Stephen
Joseph Barnabas
Peter
Nero
Constantine
Vibia Perpetua
Felicitas
Saturus
Saturninus
Revocatus
Clement
Origen
Pantaenus
Bishop Methodius
Ambrose
Arius
Athanasius
St. Augustine
Tertullian
St. John Chrysostom
St. Benedict of Nursia
St. Francis of Assisi

St. Dominic
James, the brother of Jesus
St. John of Damascus
Prince Vladimir of Kiev
St. Anselm
Michelangelo
Martin Luther
Pope Leo X
Huldrych Zwingli
Henry VIII
St. Ignatius Loyola
Alessandro Valignano
St. Teresa of Avila
Pope Pius V
John Wesley
Jonathan Edwards
Billy Graham
M.G. "Pat" Robertson
Joseph Smith
Brigham Young
Juan Luis Segundo
Bishop Desmond Tutu
James H. Cone
Rosemary Radford Ruether
Karl Barth
Cotton Mather
John Woolman
Walter Rauschenbusch
Mother Teresa

Catherine of Siena
Patriarch Cerularius
Pope Gregory the Great
Albert the Great
Pope Urban II
Pope Julius II
Tetzel
John Calvin
Wilhelm Röubli
George Fox
Francis Xavier
Matteo Ricci
St. John of the Cross
Anne Hutchinson
George Whitefield
Martin Luther King, Jr.
Oral Roberts
Mary Baker Eddy
Rev. Sun Myung Moon
Pope John XXIII
Gustavo Gutierrez
Father Naim Ateek
J. Deotis Roberts
Albert Schweitzer
Emil Brunner
St. Irenaeus
Henry Ward Beecher
Martin Luther King

C) Texts

New Testament
Sermon on the Mount
Exodus
Isaiah
Acts of the Apostles
Romans
gospel(s)
Revelation of John
Q (Quelle)
epistles
Galatians
Philemon
Ephesians
Titus
James
Jude
Gospel of Thomas

Gospel of Luke
Gospel of Mark
Gospel of Matthew
Zachariah
Torah
Corinthians (I,II)
Book of Daniel
canon
Gospel of John
Thessalonians (I,II)
Phillipians
Colossians
Timothy (I,II)
Peter (I,II)
John (I,II,III)
Hebrews
pslams

De Principiis
The Confessions
Summa Contra Gentiles
Summa Theologica
Ninety-Five Theses
Institutes of the Christian Religion
Book of Common Prayer
Spiritual Exercises
Constitutions
Science and Health with Key to the Scriptures
Book of Mormon
Nostra Aetate
apocalyptic literature
manuscripts of Nag Hammadi
Vulgate

D) Individuals and Terms From Other Traditions

Hillel
Shammai
Judaism
Passover
Hellenism
Alexander the Great
Plato
Platonism
Philo
Plotinus
Aristotle
Toyotomi Hideyoshi
Oda Nobunaga
Enlightenment
John Locke
René Descartes
Voltaire
Marxism
Manichaeanism
Nicholas Copernicus
Galileo Galilei
Sir Isaac Newton
Charles Darwin
Mohandas K. Gandhi

PART THREE GUIDED REVIEW

1. The Christian holiday of Easter is the day when Christians believe ______________________________.

2. When Jesus met his cousin John the Baptist in the gospel accounts what happened was ______________________________
______________________________.

3. Christians interpret the Hebrew Bible in light of ________
______________________________.
Jewish believers ______________ this interpretation.

4. Jesus's attitude towards the Mosaic Law could be described as ______________________________.

5. Many of Jesus's followers addressed him as ____________, which meant _______________.

6. When Jesus taught he often used a type of tale called ________________.

7. The term "Messiah" means ________________________________.

8. Many Christians believe that when Jesus and his followers ate their last supper together Jesus instituted _____________ ____________________________.

9. The New Testament contains accounts that after Jesus rose from the dead his followers saw _________________________. Christians call this rising from the dead _______________.

10. Pentecost was the day that ____________________________ ____.

11. Although Paul became the greatest champion of the new Jesus movement, for a time he ___________________________.

12. A major controversy for the early Church was the questions of whether Gentiles had to ____________________ ____.

13. Paul's attitude towards the body and sex was ___________ ____.

14. Roman Catholics believe that the first bishop of Rome was ___________________.

15. ______________ and _____________ were the young mother and her slave who choose martyrdom over renouncing their faith.

16. The persecution of the Christians in the Roman Empire ended when ___________________ made Christianity a legal religion.

17. Scholars believe that the earliest of the four Gospel accounts to be written was ___________________.

18. The Gospel accounts of <u>Matthew</u> and <u>Luke</u>, many scholars believe, were based in part on the writings _____________ and _______________, and possibly others.

19. The Gospels were probably written sometime after _______.

20. The oldest texts in the New Testament are those written by ____________________, which are in the form of ______________________.

21. A major influence upon early Christian thinkers such as Origen was ______________________. The method that many of these thinkers used is termed the ________________ method.

22. One teaching of Origen that was rejected later by the Church was his belief that ___________________________.

23. The council at Nicea rejected the position of the Arians who believed that ___________________________________.

24. The Greek term homoousia means _____________________ ________________________________.

25. The Council of Chalcedon took the position that Jesus was ____.

26. The Roman Catholic and Orthodox traditions disagreed over the question of whether the Holy Spirit ________________ ____.

27. Augustine and Pelagius disagreed over the question of ____.
Augustine's position was ___________________________.

28. Three famous religious orders were those of the ________________, the _____________________ and the _______________________.

29. One difference between the Roman Catholic and Orthodox traditions is their use of religious symbols; the Orthodox tradition makes great use of _______________.

30. The approach that developed in the schools of France in the eleventh century and that applied logic to theological questions was called ____________________.

31. Thomas Aquinas believed that some truths concerning God could be accepted by using either _______________ or __________________.

32. Despite the fact that the Crusades were supposed to attack Muslims, in fact much violence was also committed against ________________and__________________.

33. The three main Protestant divisions from Rome during the Reformation were those of ___________________, __________________ and ______________________.

3. Which of the following is <u>not</u> one of the canonical gospels?

   a. Luke
   b. John
   c. Mark
   d. Thomas

4. The Society of Friends was founded by

   a. William Penn
   b. Ignatius Loyola
   c. Francis Xavier
   d. George Fox

5. Which of the following would Luther recognize as a sacrament?

   a. Confirmation
   b. Holy Orders
   c. Baptism
   d. Marriage

6. The group that believed that Christ was the highest and best creature made by God was the

   a. Arians
   b. Adoptionists
   c. Monophysites
   d. Pelagians

7. The Christian Church is believed to have begun on the day called

   a. Christmas.
   b. Pentecost.
   c. Easter.
   d. Good Friday.

8. Which of the following is the traditional Christian position concerning life after death?

   a. Immortality of the soul
   b. Reincarnation
   c. Resurrection of the dead.
   d. Resurrection of the spirit only.

9. The founder of the Jesuit order was

   a. St. Francis.
   b. St. Benedict.
   c. St. Ignatius Loyola.
   d. St. Thomas Aquinas.

10. The type of story that Jesus often used in his teachings is

   a. Folk tales.
   b. Myths.
   c. Legends.
   d. Parables.

C) <u>True-False</u>

T F 1. The followers of Jesus during his lifetime called Jesus by the title "rabbi."

T F 2. St. Thomas Aquinas shifted Christian theology from Aristotelianism to Platonism.

T F 3. The term "Messiah" means "the anointed of God."

T F 4. Prior to the Second Vatican Council all Roman Catholic translations of the Bible were done from the Septuagint.

T F 5. Many scholars believe that the Gospel to Matthew was written by reference to "Q".

T F 6. Jesus of Nazareth rejected completely Mosaic Law.

T F 7. The Christian term "Kerygma" refers to the healing power of Jesus.

T F 8. The Council of Chalcedon sided with the Monophysites on the question concerning the nature of Jesus Christ.

T F 9. John Calvin stressed that humans can not save themselves through doing good deeds.

T F 10. The Gospel According to John is usually viewed as giving an account of the life of Jesus independent from the other gospels.

PART SIX ESSAY AND DISCUSSION QUESTIONS

1. Compare Martin Luther's and John Calvin's view of the salvation process and the role of the Church to the Roman Catholic view.

2. Describe Paul's view of sex, love and women. What influence do you think Paul's position on these questions had on later Christian thought?

3. Compare and contrast the view of Mosaic Law in Rabbinic Judaism, in Jesus's teachings and in Paul's teachings (refer to Text Three above.) For each of them, how does Torah figure in God's plan for mankind? Is Paul's position the same as the position of Jesus?

4. Explain the process by which the gospels were formed. How might this process raise issues concerning the nature and authority of scripture?

5. Summarize Aquinas's attempt to prove the existence of God through an analysis of motion. Is Aquinas's argument a sound one? Why or why not? What does an argument of this type illustrate about how Aquinas believed man could approach God?

6. Explain the development of Christology (the study of who Jesus was) from the New Testament writings until the Council of Chalcedon.

PART SEVEN CONFRONTING ISSUES AND ANSWERS

The question of the role of women and how religious traditions should change their view of the role of women is an issue that confronts all of the major world religions. A variety of factors, however, make this an especially contentious issue in Christianity. The multitude of different denominations and sects within Christianity means that there can be no unified response to this issue; different groups will address the issue in different ways. The greater overall status of women in Western culture leads many women with Christian beliefs to demand that they achieve complete equality with men in the Church. In addition, according to the interpretation of many Christians, there are passages in the New Testament that appear to give women a different, and, perhaps, lesser role than men. For example, Paul exhorted: "Wives, be subject to your husbands; that is your Christian duty. Husbands, love your wives and do not be harsh with them"(Colossians III:18).

Think about the role of women in Christianity in reference to two questions. First, what might be the sources of authority that different Christians might use to resolve this question? Which Christian branches might emphasize which sources? Might there be problems in determining exactly what the position of an authority might be on the role of women? For example, if one held that the Bible is the ultimate authority, what problems might there be in determining what the Bible has to say on the role of women? Second, to what degree can the role of women change as the social and historical circumstances change? Could the proper Christian role for women at the time of Jesus be different than the proper Christian role at the beginning of the Twenty-First century? Will ones answer to this question be dependent on one's view of the source of authority?

PART EIGHT AN ESSAY FOR DEEPER CONSIDERATION

Essay Question

Compare the Christian belief in resurrection of the dead to Plato's belief in immortality of the soul, and the Hindu belief in Atman and reincarnation. Where are these beliefs similar and where are they different?

Tips for Answering

In a previous "Essay for Deeper Consideration" section you were asked to write a comparison essay. A number of tips were given on how you might structure a comparison essay. In many cases, however, before you can present a comparison to your readers, you may need to consider a number of related or underlying issues. This essay question illustrates some of these issues, and how you could address them in your essay. You would not want to raise all these questions in any one essay; you rather should consider how each relates to the thesis around which you want to structure your writing.

You might decide to begin by defining and clarifying each of the three concepts of life after death. After all, before you can compare the three views you will need to explicate each view for your readers. Each of the three positions is a complex belief. The Hindu position on reincarnation, for example, can not be understood apart from the theory of the Atman. Within the course of explaining reincarnation you would need to define "Atman" and explain the role of Atman in Hindu belief. Similarly, in order to understand the concept of resurrection of the dead it is necessary to address the issue of what is resurrected. Theoretically, one could believe in the resurrection of different elements of the human being (e.g. body, mind, spirit, some combination of these). According to Christian understanding, what is the nature of the resurrected person? Furthermore, what does the answer to this question reveal about the Christian view of the nature of the human person? Obviously, in your essay you can not address fully every relevant topic. However, you will need to be aware of these issues, and will need to decide which of these questions need to be raised and answered in the course of explicating each positions.

You might also address the issue of how ideas from different cultures can be compared. The essay question might assume that a comparison between these three positions is not problematic. Is this the case? These three views were adopted in three very different cultural milieus: the early Christian movement, Greece and India. Language, ideas, worldviews - all these are shaped by one's culture. In each case, how was the position on life after death reflective of and shaped by the culture? A further aspect of this question is the degree to which apparent differences in the three positions merely reflect different ways different cultures express the same idea. To what degree are the divergences between these three positions differences in the way in which the beliefs are expressed, and to what degree are they differences in what the beliefs express? Finally, you might raise the more fundamental issue of the validity of such a comparison. Can each position only be understood and analyzed in terms of its own worldview and culture? This is a fairly radical position, but you might believe that the issue needs to be examined prior to a comparison of the views.

PART NINE PROJECTS FOR DEVELOPING RELIGIOUS EMPATHY

1. Many Christians find in "The Sermon on the Mount" one of the most beautiful and clearest descriptions of the

Christian life. In this passage Jesus gives his closest disciples both general values and principles to live by, and specific injunctions and prohibitions. Many scholars believe that the author of The Gospel According to Matthew gathered together talks given by Jesus at different times, and combined them in this one passage. Scholars have also commented on the manner in which this gospel distinguishes between teachings for the public, and teachings for the disciples. The Sermon would seem to belong to the latter category. Finally, the fact that the author chooses to portray Jesus as giving this speech on a hill could be an attempt to draw a connection between Moses, Mount Sinai and the Law, on the one hand, and Jesus, the hill and a new view of Law. All these factors suggest that for the author of this gospel, and for Christians since, Jesus's talk should be a guide for Christians on how to live.

Read the Sermon on the Mount in a modern translation of The Gospel According to Matthew (Matthew V-VII). (You might also want to compare this version of the Sermon with the version found in The Gospel According to Luke beginning at VI:17.) What do you think Jesus is asking of his followers? Imagine that you were trying to live according to what Jesus says in this passage, how would you have to live your life? What changes, if any, would you have to make in your life? Are there things that you do or believe in with which Jesus would disagree? Try to imagine one day lived in accord with this sermon. Specifically, what would such a day be like?

2. A religion expresses itself in its houses of worship, both inside and outside. Church buildings are, in part, the attempt to express in architecture some of the beliefs of Christianity. Close observation and analysis of different church buildings can tell you a lot about Christian beliefs. It can also serve as an indication of how different denominations and groups see the Christian message.

   Together with a fellow student or a friend, compile a list of different churches in your town or city. Include on your list any famous churches, and any church buildings that you know to be architecturally important. If your city has a Roman Catholic or Episcopal Cathedral (the principal church of the bishop's see) include it on your list. Try to put on your list churches that reflect a wide variety of Christian denominations (a meeting house of the Society of Friends, a Unitarian church, a Baptist church, a Black Pentecostal storefront church, etc.) Your selection will be influenced by the diversity of religious groups in your town, and the physical proximity of the different buildings.

After you have compiled your list, take a walking tour with your companion. When you get to each building notice the particulars of the architecture: What is the physical location of the building? What is the relation between the physical location of the building, and the size and scope of the building? How would you describe the building's shape? Are there any ornaments on the outside of the building, and if so, what are they? Would you describe the building as simple, or ornate? Out of which materials is the building made, and how does this influence the aesthetic of the building? After you have noted these features, consider how they might reflect the Christian message as this church interprets it: What values might a simple building or an ornate building express? What message might be given by putting a church on top of a hill? Would this differ from building a church in amongst homes and businesses? How could you express architecturally the concept of being open to all people? How could you express the concept of the importance of God?

3. For Christians a church is more than a building. A church is also the community of believers in Christ. You might want to visit, with a friend, a number of different Christian congregations and observe their worship and fellowship. If you feel you would like to do this, try to visit at least two congregations from different parts of the Christian spectrum. If you are going to visit a large urban church, you will probably not have to talk to the minister or priest beforehand. However, if you plan to visit a small congregation, it would be best to contact the minister prior to your actual visit. Explain that you are taking a course in World Religions, and as part of a class project you would like to observe a variety of Christian denominations. You should also communicate that, while you are a student of religion, you are not seeking to join any particular group. If the minister does not feel comfortable with your visit, you should not visit that particular group.

   When you visit each service, observe how each group expresses its religious beliefs in worship. What are the practices of each group? What is the relation (both physically and organizationally) of the clergy or leader to the group as a whole? What appear to be the most important portions of the service? If you were summarizing the service like a drama, when does the climax occur? What is the emotional feeling during the service: excited, calm, reflective, anxious? What conclusions can you draw concerning each group based on your observation of their religious rituals?

ANSWER KEY TO SELF-TEST

B) Multiple Choice

1. c	6. a
2. a	7. b
3. d	8. c
4. d	9. c
5. c	10. d

C) True-False

1. T	6. F
2. F	7. F
3. T	8. F
4. F	9. T
5. T	10. T

Notes

[1]Martin Luther, "On the Babylonish Captivity of the Church," First Principles of the Reformation, trans. H. Wace and C. A. Buchheim (Philadelphia: Lutheran Publication Society; 1885) 232.

[2]The Gospel According to Mark, XIII:28-31, The New English Bible (Oxford: Oxford University Press, 1970)

[3]St. Paul, The Letter of Paul to the Romans, III: 21-25, The New English Bible (Oxford: Oxford University Press, 1970).

Chapter 10
Islam

PART ONE LEARNING OBJECTIVES

Doing these exercises, in conjunction with reading the textbook, should help you to achieve the following objectives. Read them and see how many you already have mastered; then study the following terms and concepts, and work through the exercises. After you have completed all the exercises, return to this section and review the objectives again.

You should be able to:

1. Describe the Muslim hajj, and indicate its significance for Islam.

2. Relate the life of Muhammad, explain his role as prophet and messenger in Islam, and illustrate the importance of Muhammad as a role-model for Muslims.

3. Explain and analyze the role of the Quran for Islam, and compare and contrast Islam's view of the Quran to the view of scripture in other religious traditions.

4. Analyze the organizational development of Islam during the time of the first four caliphs, and indicate how events during this period influenced Islam at a later date.

5. Describe and analyze the differences between the Shia and the Sunni branches of Islam, and indicate the effect this split has on the Islamic world today.

6. Discuss the notion of the shari'a, name and explain at least four standards that can be used to interpret law, and name and describe the four different schools of Islamic legal interpretation.

7. Cite some of the Greek influences on Islam, and illustrate how some of these influences were reflected in Islamic philosophy.

8. Examine the role of mysticism in Islam, in particular, discussing the Sufi movement, and orthodox Islam's reaction to this movement.

9. Summarize the position of Al-Ghazali, and indicate his influence upon subsequent Islamic thought and practice.

10. Discuss the history of Islam's relation to other religions, including the relation between Muhammad and the Jewish population in Medina, the Crusades, Islam's influence on Medieval Christian theologians, and contemporary relations between Islam and other religions.

11. Examine and write about the problem of Islam and Modernism, citing some examples of different Islamic responses to this problem.

12. Outline the history of Islam in the United States, focusing on its history in the Midwest and on the East Coast, and the history of the Black Muslim movement.

13. Discuss and write about the Islamic Worldview; in particular, the Islamic view of the Absolute, the world, the human role, the fundamental problem and resolution for human beings, community and ethics, rituals and symbols, life after death, and other religions.

14. Analyze and synthesize various views on fundamentalism in Islam and other religions, and formulate in writing a comprehensive understanding of fundamentalism.

PART TWO TERMS AND INDIVIDUALS

A) Terms and Concepts

Islam	Muslims
Allah (God)	Quran
People of the Book	shari'a
ka'bah	angel Gabriel
Quraysh tribe	hanif
Medina (Yathrib)	jinn
Hijrah	ansar
muhajirun	Ummayads
Khazraj	Aws
Hawazin	Thaquf
monotheism	Shahada
rasul	surah
zakat	Ramadan
Tawhid	salat
mosque	rak'as
muezzin	Sunna
jizyah	hadith
caliph	shi'a
Sunni	Kharijites
imam	Twelvers
Mahdi	Zaydis
hujjah	hisàb
Ismailis	Mogul Empire
dhimmi	Shari'a
ijma	ulama
qiyas	Hanifite school
ra'y	Malikite school
Shafiite school	Hanbalite
Murjites	Mu'tazilites
Sufis	peoples of the Book
Crusades	Saladin
Taj Mahal	madrasas
Wahhabi	Salifiya
ummah	Muslim Brotherhood
pan-Islam	al-Azhar
Federation of Islamic Associations	
Muslim World League	Muslim Student Associations
Islamic Society of North America	
Black Muslim Movement	American Muslim Mission
Nation of Islam	Iblis
Adam	Eve
Satan	mihrab
Mecca (Makkah)	Ka'bah
kiswah	ihram
Hajj	hajji

hajjiyah
revelation (wahy)
zar ceremonies
Islamic fundamentalism

B) Individuals

Muhammad
Abraham
Hagar
Ishmael
Sarah
Isaac
Abdullah
Aminah
Halimah
Abu Talib
Khadijah
Zaynab
Ruqayyah
Umm-Khulthum
Katima
Waraqa Ibn-Nawfal
Zayd Ibn Horithah
Ali
Abu Bakr
Khalid Ibn Said
Uthman Ibn Affan
Aishah
Abu Sufyan
Khalid Ibn al-Walid
Zaynab Bint al-Harith
Zayd Ibn Thabit
Abu Bakr
Aishah
Umar
Uthman
Mu'awiyah
Hasan
Husayn
Muhammad al-Mahdi
Zayd
Ismail
Musa al-Kazim
Usamah
Akbar
Babur
Hanbal
Al-Shafi
Al-Ashari
Al-Ghazali
Ibn Arabi
Rabia
Al-Din Rumi
Al-Hallaj
Al-Farabi
Ibn Sina
Ibn Arabi
Beha-ed-Din
Ibn Rushd (Averroës)
Shah Jahan
Muhammad Ibn Abd al-Wahhab
Rashid Rida
Jamil-al-Din al-Afghani
Abd al-Hamid II
Muhammad Abduh
Sayyid Ahmad Khan
Amir Ali
Sir Muhammad Iqbal
Abul Ala Mawdudi
Zia ul-Haq
Benazir Bhutto
Gammel Abdel Nasser
Sayyid Qutb
Anwar Sadat
Hasni Mubarak
Muammar al-Qaddafi
Yasir Arafat
Ruhullah Khomeini
Hashemi Rafsanjani
Elijah Muhammad
Malcolm X
Wallace Dean Muhammad
Louis Farrakhan (Louis X)
Muhammad Ahmad
Hasan al-Banna

C) Texts

Quran
Sunna

The Spirit of Islam
Green Book
hadiths

D) Individuals and Terms from Other Traditions

Judaism
Christianity
Byzantine
Charles Martel
Buddhism
Neoplatonism
Gnosticism
materialists
naturalists
theists
Plato
Aristotle
New Testament
Son of God
Trinity
patriarch of Constantinople
Pope Urban II
Alexius I
Frederick II
Holy Roman Empire
Richard I
Maimonides
St. Thomas Aquinas
Albertus Magnus
Sikhism
Nicolaus Copernicus
Charles Darwin
Henri Bergson
Fredrich Nietzsche
Alfred North Whitehead
Greek Orthodox Christianity
Israel
Abu al-Hakam
Baha'i
Baha'u'llah

PART THREE GUIDED REVIEW

1. Islam dates from the ______________ century C.E.

2. According to Islam the final prophet of God is _________ __________________.

3. The series of revelations received from God is the _________.

4. The ritual and ethical laws governing the lives of Muslims is called the _________________.

5. At the time Muhammad was born, inside the Ka'bah there were ______________________.

6. ______________________ was the wife of Muhammad, and his counselor.

7. While meditating in a cave, Muhammad was given a message from _______________, delivered by ______________________. At first Muhammad was afraid that he was _________________ ______________________.

8. The <u>Hijrah</u> was ______________________________________.

9. The city to which Muhammad moved, Yathrib, is today called ____________________. It was while he was here that friction began to develop between Muhammad and his followers, and __________________________.

10. The five requirements that are made of every Muslim are: a) ____________________________________, b) _____________ ______________________________, c) _____________________ _______________________, d) _____________________________ and e) ____.

11. <u>Tawhid</u> is ____.

12. Islam rejects the Christian beliefs that ________________ ____.

13. The two chief sources of authority in Islam are, first, the Quran, and after this, _______________________________.

14. One difference between the <u>Shia</u> and the <u>Sunni</u> is over their understanding of _______________________________. According to the Shia, Ali was the first __________________.

15. The group known as the Twelvers believe that ___________ ____. They believe that the <u>Mahdi</u> will ____.

16. The Muslim expansion into Europe was finally turned back by _________________________.

17. The term <u>Shari'a</u> means ________________________. According to different schools, this might involve _________________, ____________________, _________________, and even _______________________.

18. The legal school known as the Hanbalite School could be described as ______________________________. It is prevalent in the country of ___________________________.

19. The position of the Mu'tazilites was ____________________ ____.

20. The name "Sufi" is taken from __________________________.

21. The Persian Sufi Al-Hallaj was __________________________ __________________________________.

22. Al-Ghazali thought that Aristotle and Plato ____________
____.

23. According to Ibn Arabi, everything that we experience is
____.

24. While Jews and Christians were not forced to convert to Islam, they were made to _________________________________.

25. The Crusades were undertaken with the goal of __________
____.

26. Ibn Rushd is better known in the West as _______________. He was famous for his commentaries on the works of _________ _______________, which were studied by ______________________.

27. The Taj Mahal was built as a ___________________________.

28. The movement known as Wahhabi stresses __________________
____.

29. Amir Ali argued that Muhammad was ______________________
_______________________________________.

30. Sir Muhammad Iqbal is noteworthy for both _____________ ___________________________________ and for ________________
_______________________________________.

31. The views of ___________________________ on the Islamic State were expressed in <u>The Green Book</u>.

32. One of the most important recent events in the Islamic world was the return of ________________________ to Iran in 1979.

33. The two major groups that represent Islam in the United States are ____________________ and ______________________.

34. The founder of the Nation of Islam was _______________.

35. Islam's views on the issue of The Absolute can be described as a position of ___________________. For Islam the only God is ____________.

36. Islam interprets the story of Adam and Eve to mean _____
____.

37. The term for a Muslim community is _______________.

38. Islam's view on marriage is ______________________________.
Islam's view of divorce is ________________________________.

39. Mosques have a <u>mihrab</u> so that ____________________________.

40. The holy city that all Muslims face in prayer __________ times a day is __________________.

41. The Ka'bah is a _____________________________________.
It is usually covered with a __________________.

42. Inside the Ka'bah is a ________________________. Muslims believe that this was given by _________________ to ________ _______________.

43. During the time one participates in the <u>hajj</u> one is in a state of ________________. A male who completes the <u>hajj</u> is called a ________________, a female a __________________.

44. Islam's view on life after death is ____________________ ____.

45. A. J. Arberry views revelation in the Quran as _______ ____.

46. Martin E. Marty sees "fundamentalism" as having the characteristics of ____.

PART FOUR ANALYZING TEXTS

Below are three texts that were not in the textbook. The texts, however, do contain ideas and concepts with which you should be familiar after reading the textbook and studying the selections in the textbook from primary religious documents. Read each text carefully, compare it to the primary documents you have studied and try to analyze each by answering the following questions: What are the main ideas in the text? What viewpoint or viewpoints might the author of the text represent? Is it possible to identify the specific thinker, discipline, movement, tradition or work from which the text derives? What intellectual, literary, social, cultural or historical influences are reflected in the text? For each of your conclusions, try to point to specific evidence in the text (e.g. terms, ideas, arguments, writing style, etc.) which supports your conclusion. Be careful that your conclusions do not exceed the evidence upon which they rest.

TEXT ONE

Know that the key of happiness is following the Sunna and imitating God's Apostle in all his goings out and comings in, in his movements and times of quiescence, even in the manner of his eating, his deportment, his sleep and his speech. I do not say that concerning his manners in matters of religious observances alone, because there is no reason to neglect the traditions which have come down concerning them: nay, that has to do with all matters of use and wont, for in that way unrestricted following arises. . . Muhammad b. Aslam used not to eat a melon because the manner in which God's Apostle ate it had not been transmitted to him.[1]

TEXT TWO

Say: "O mankind, I am Allah's messenger to you all,
Of Him to whom belongeth the kingdom of the heavens
and of the earth.

There is no god but He.
He giveth life and he causeth to die.
Believe then in Allah, and in His messenger,
The ummi prophet, who himself believeth in Allah
and His words, and follow him;
Haply so ye will be guided.[2]

TEXT THREE

I died as a mineral and became a plant,
I died as a plant and rose to animal,
I died as animal and I was man.
Why should I fear? When was I less by dying?
Yet once more I shall die as man, to soar
With angels blest; but even from angelhood
I must pass on: all except God doth perish.
When I have sacrificed my angel soul,
I shall become what no mind e'er conceived.
Oh, let me not exist! for Non-existence
Proclaims in organ tones, "To Him we shall return."[3]

PART FIVE SELF-TEST

A) Definitions and Descriptions - Write your own definition or description of each of the following terms, individuals or texts. After completing the self-test, check your answer with the definition or description given in the textbook.

1. Tawhid ____
____
____.

2. Ramadan ____
____
____.

3. Wahhabi ____
____
____.

4. jinn ____
____
____.

5. hajj ____
____
____.

6. surah ____
____
____.

7. imam ____
____
____.

8. Shia ____
____
____.

9. zakat ____
____
____.

10. Islam ____
____
____.

B) Multiple Choice

1. Which of the following is not mentioned as one of the considerations in determining Shari'a?

   a. Quran
   b. qiyas
   c. ijma'
   d. salat

2. According to Shia the first imam was

   a. Ali
   b. Abu Bakr
   c. Mu'awiyah
   d. Muhammad al-Mahdi

3. A male who has completed the pilgrimage to Mecca is called a

   a. hajj
   b. hajjiyah
   c. hajji
   d. ihram

4. A tradition of the prophet is called

   a. ijma'.
   b. ulama.
   c. hadith.
   d. giya.

5. The tomb of Muhammad is located in

   a. Mecca.
   b. Medina.
   c. Baghdad.
   d. Jerusalem.

6. Muhammad was from the house of

   a. Ummayad.
   b. Quraysh.
   c. Hashim.
   d. Aws.

7. Which of these is not one of the Five Pillars of Islam?

   a. Pay a tax to the needy.
   b. Fast during Ramadan.
   c. Declare the Shahada.
   d. Read the Hadiths.

8. Which of the following is not mentioned as a difference between the Shi'ites and the Sunnis?

   a. The need for a pilgrimage to Mecca.
   b. The role of family relationships in choosing the successors to Muhammad.
   c. The role of the imam.
   d. The role of Ali.

9. The sacred building pilgrims walk around in Mecca is called

   a. Kiswah.
   b. Ka'bah.
   c. The Dome of the Rock.
   d. The Tomb of the Prophet.

10. The main Shia group is called

   a. Zaydis.
   b. Twelvers.
   c. Ismailis.
   d. Kharijites.

C) <u>True-False</u>

T F 1. The Hanbalite school is the most conservative of the legal schools.

T F 2. Friction between Muslims and Jews developed soon after Muhammad moved to Medina.

T F 3. The Zaydis believe that Husayn was the proper fourth imam.

T F 4. Ibn Arabi conceived of God as the only reality in the universe.

T F 5. The concept of Tawhid means that there are gods who were created by Allah before he created the earth.

T F 6. Muslims are required to pray in a group of at least six people.

T F 7. The state of purity a Muslim must maintain during the hajj is called ihram.

T F 8. Rabia was a famous Sufi mystic.

T F 9. The angel who delivered a message from God Muhammad was the angel Moroni.

T F 10. Every Christian who lived in an area conquered by Islam had to convert to Islam.

PART SIX ESSAY AND DISCUSSION QUESTIONS

1. How would you describe Muhammad as a person? How would you contrast his role and personality to that of some of the other major religious figures you have studied (Jesus, Buddha, Confucius)?

2. Address the issue of how Islam has viewed the relation between state and religion? What have been some of the attempts to realize an Islamic state, and how have these attempts differed?

3. Explain the differences between the Sunni and the Shia branches of Islam.

4. Describe the Sufi movement, and examine how it both differs from and resembles non-mystical forms of Islam.

5. What role has Greek philosophy played in Islamic thought? How might aspects of Islamic thought differ from the way Greek thinkers like Aristotle and Plato looked at the world?

6. Examine the role that Islam has played in the Middle East since the 1967 Arab-Israeli War. What might be its future role in the region?

PART SEVEN CONFRONTING ISSUES AND ANSWERS

All the major world religions are facing the challenge of adapting to the modern world. Scientific advances, demands on the part of women for greater equality, economic changes that are influencing the family and the individual - all these are factors each religion must address. In this regard, Islam is no different than most of the world's religions. Certain Islamic countries have strove to maintain or restore traditional Islamic values and practices; Saudi Arabia and Iran would be two such countries. The result has been a greater sense of frustration on the part of Muslims in those countries that want modernization, and a greater sense of determination on behalf of those who mean to resist it. As the textbook describes it, this is in part a tension between modernization and fundamentalism.

The question of modernization and fundamentalism in Islam, however, is not a simple issue. Modernization in certain areas is seen as relatively problem free; modernization in other areas is strictly forbidden. As with many other religious traditions, moreover, the prohibitions in some areas are not rooted in scripture itself, but rather in tradition and interpretation. A recent example of this occurred in Saudi Arabia during the Fall of 1990 at the time of the Gulf War. Women are strictly forbidden to drive in Saudi Arabia. Influenced, perhaps, by the presence of American servicewomen driving in their country, a group of Saudi Arabian women got behind the wheels of their cars and drove through the streets of Riyadh. The women were stopped and taken into custody. They were later suspended from their teaching positions. Much of public opinion in the country condemned the women's actions. The fascinating aspect of this case, however, is the following. At the time of this incident it was not strictly illegal for the women to drive. Moreover, the Islamic scholars were in agreement that the Quran did not prohibit women from driving. Rather, the argument against women driving was based on tradition and a general belief concerning the proper role for women in an Islamic society.

Consider this incident from the standpoint of an Islamic legal scholar. To what sources of authority might each side of this issue appeal? Which sources would most likely be given greater weight, and which might be give lesser or no weight? How would the various schools of interpretation differ in which sources they used? Would this specific incident raise any special problems for reaching a decision (e.g.. would it matter if it had occurred during a war?) Which school of interpretation would best be able to make adjustments to modernization?

PART EIGHT AN ESSAY FOR DEEPER CONSIDERATION

Essay Question

Judaism, Christianity and Islam have each been called "revealed-historical religions." Examine examples of "divine revelation" in the Jewish, Christian and Islamic traditions. Is it possible to synthesize the different examples of revelation into a general Judeo-Christian-Islamic understanding of revelation? Or is it possible to define a variety of approaches to understanding revelation ("fundamentalist", "critical", etc.) What would such understandings look like?

Tips for Answering

This essay question assumes that you have already read the chapters on Judaism and Christianity, and have discussed those chapters in class. If this is not the case, you may need to postpone working on this essay until you have studied those traditions.

When you "analyze" something you break it down into its component parts; when you "synthesize" something you draw together parts in order to construct a new whole. The task of "synthesis" is being defined in this essay assignment, however, in a way that may differ from how it is defined in some English classes. For example, a recent composition textbook defines "synthesis" as when ". . . you take several separate sources of information - a group of statements, a collection of essays - and you analyze each individual point of view and each way of looking at the topic. . . [you] incorporate them all in a new essay designed to represent a variety of opinion as well as your own point of view." [4] In one sense, of course, you are being asked to do some of this in this essay. You will need to select examples of God's revelation from each of the three traditions. You will also want to analyze each individual example in order to illuminate how each tradition understands the phenomenon of revelatory experiences. But you are also being asked to do something different than the type of synthesis mentioned in the quotation. You are not merely being asked to incorporate them into a new essay. You are being challenged to uncover common structures or elements in all three that would allow you to draw together a new understanding of revelation for all three traditions. Do the three traditions share a common view of revelation, and if so, what is that view? Answering this question should be your overall goal in writing the essay.

Here are a few more suggestions to take into consideration. The textbook discusses the views of different representatives of each tradition on revelation. You should not merely repeat either of these views in your essay, but they might provide you with models for a general theory of revelation. Also, when you choose your examples from each tradition, make sure you are choosing a "paradigm case". That is to say, each tradition contains unusual or controversial cases of revelatory experiences. An example in Islam might be the revelation to Al-Hallaj. Such borderline cases have limited usefulness in deriving a general understanding of the concept. A widely accepted example, such as the revelation of the Quran to Muhammad, would be more useful. Finally, notice that the question leaves open the possibility that you will conclude that such a general understanding does not exist. If your analysis shows this, do not be afraid to argue that position.

PART NINE PROJECTS FOR DEVELOPING RELIGIOUS EMPATHY

1. The projects suggested in this section of each chapter are not designed to convert you to any particular religion, or to encourage you to practice any religion. That is a matter for each individual to decide apart from a college course on religious studies. These projects, however, are formulated to get you to understand and empathize with each of the religious traditions. One aspect of Islam that many scholars have commented on is how rituals structure time for a Muslim. Consider a few of the Five Pillars, the obligations on all believers. The obligation to witness is constant. Prayer structures each day into five periods. The year revolves around Ramadan, and in a sense, the lifetime revolves around the pilgrimage. Thus, practice or action helps to define time as God's time.

   To get a sense of how time can be structured, and how this might change the way in which we see the world, try the following. Choose five convenient times that are equally distributed throughout the day and evening. For at least three or four days try to stop whatever you are doing during these times and spend five minutes on some quiet reflection. If you normally pray in some way, you might want to pray during these times. But if you do not pray, then use them to examine a thought or to quietly think. (Realize, of course, that for Islam, the crucial aspect of these times is to witness to God. Any other use of the times is significantly different.) Make them in some way special times. When you have done this for a few days, consider: How does doing this change the way in which you go through your day? Is it a bother, one that takes time away from your studies or partying? Or do you look forward to it, as a break or a refreshing moment? Given our society, are such breaks practical? Are they valuable because they are not practical? What has this shown you about Islamic practice?

2. The Middle East and Iran, and with it Islam, have been in the news constantly over the past ten years. Given the geo-political realities of the region, it would appear to be a safe prediction that Islam will continue to be a focus of attention for years to come. While many of the reasons for this attention are unfortunate ones, and may have little to do with the beliefs and practices of Islam itself, it does give you an opportunity to learn about the religion and the attitude of Americans towards it.

   Begin to keep a scrapbook of newspaper clippings dealing with Islam and countries that are predominantly Islamic. Cut out the relevant ones, and paste them in the book. Write a short reflection on each clipping. Try to focus on two issues. First, what do the accounts show you about how Muslims view and try to achieve an Islamic state? Which countries are mentioned as "Islamic" countries? What do you think that means? What form of government do these countries have (monarchy, democracy, oligarchy, theocracy, etc.)? What view of an Islamic state do other groups in the Middle East have? Second, what do these articles show you about Americans' knowledge of and opinion of Islam? Does it seem well-informed, unbiased? Or does it seem ignorant and prejudiced? If you find prejudice in some accounts, how is this manifested? Should Americans try to learn more about Islam?

ANSWER KEY TO SELF-TEST

B) Multiple Choice

1. d	6. c
2. a	7. d
3. c	8. a
4. c	9. b
5. b	10. b

C) True-False

1. T	6. F
2. T	7. T
3. F	8. T
4. T	9. F
5. F	10. F

Notes

[1]Al-Ghazali, in James Robson, "Al-Ghazali and the Sunna", The Muslim World, Oct. 1955, Vol. 45, No. 4: 324-333.

[2]Quran, 7:157-8, quoted in Philip K. Hitti, Islam: A Way of Life (Chicago: Henery Regnery Company, 1970) 10.

[3]Al-Rumi, Islam: A Way of Life, Philip Hitti (Chicago: Henry Regnery Company, 1970) 62-63.

[4]Brenda Spatt, Writing from Sources, 3rd Ed. (New York: St. Martin's Press, 1991) 223.

CONCLUSION

PART ONE   LEARNING OBJECTIVES

Doing these exercises, in conjunction with reading the textbook, should help you to achieve the following objectives. Read them and see how many you already have mastered; then study the following terms and concepts, and work through the exercises. After you have completed all the exercises, return to this section and review the objectives again.

You should be able to:

1. Explain and clarify the tension between divergence and convergence, between maintaining a rich diversity and finding a common ground in the study of world religions.

2. Name and illustrate at least three different approaches to addressing the issue of convergence and divergence among world religions, and give examples from the thought of at least three different scholars of religion.

3. List and illustrate at least three ways you could learn more about peoples from other faiths.

PART TWO TERMS AND INDIVIDUALS

A) Terms and Concepts

sacred
diversity
exoteric
phenomenal
faith
sacred space
sacred nature
sacred human life
worldview
shared experience
esoteric
noumenal
sacred time
myths
sacred cosmos
dialogue

B) Individuals

Ramakrishna
Frithjof Schuon
Immanuel Kant
Mircea Eliade
Huston Smith
John Hick
Wilfred Cantwell Smith

PART THREE GUIDED REVIEW

1. The problem of diversity and common ground could be defined as ______________________________.

2. The textbook presents you with __________ different approaches to this problem.

3. Ramakrishna represents the position that ________________ ______________________________.

4. Three thinkers who belong to the second group and take the position that at an ideal level religions agree on one Absolute are ________________, ____________________, and ________________.

5. The position of the second group rests on the distinction between the __________ level of a religion's teaching and the _____________ level of that teaching.

6. The thought of Wilfred Cantwell Smith centers around the term ___________, which means for him __________________.

7. The third approach is represented by _________________. This group believes that ________________________________.

8. Three ways one can learn more about the faiths of other people are through ____________________, __________________, and ________________________.

PART FOUR ESSAY QUESTION FOR CONTINUING REFLECTION

Essay question

If it is now the end of term, you will have read many selections from the primary documents of world religions and will have read major portions of the textbook. If you have worked hard you will know much more about religion than you did at the start of the term. Some of the ideas you had about what religious people believe or do may have been illustrated and clarified. Other ideas may have been disproved or cast aside. It might be interesting, therefore, for you to think and write about how you view "religion" at this milepost in your study, and how, or if, your thinking on this "Religion" has changed in the past few months.

Write an essay in which you reformulate your general definition of "Religion". After stating your definition, explain why you believe this to be the most useful definition for understanding different world religions, explain how your definition has changed, and illustrate how your definition would apply (or not apply) to at least three of the religious traditions you have studied this semester.

Tips for answering:

If you formulated a definition of "religion" during the first few weeks of the semester (as suggested in the Introduction to this book), go back and revisit this definition. Consider whether you still agree with your approach in the earlier definition. Consider the following questions: Would you still define "religion" in the same manner? How would your definition have to change based on your study? Why do you feel it needs to be modified? Or do you think your original definition has been confirmed and deepened?

Based on your answers to these questions, begin to rethink and rework your definition. In thinking through this issue, consider all the material you have studied this semester: in the textbook, in the study guide, in all the primary documents you have read, in the lectures by your professor, and in discussion in the classroom, with friends and with family. Notice that the essay question asks you to explain why your definition would be helpful in understanding "Religion" and religious traditions. Again, there are a number of ways in which you could approach this task. The textbook Introduction there are critiques of the proposals by Clark and Tillich; these critiques try to apply these definitions to religious traditions such as Judaism and Buddhism. You probably should use a similar approach. After brainstorming the issue, gradually begin modifying or reworking your original definition.

When you have arrived at a satisfactory revision of your definition, try testing it out against the different traditions you have studied. In your essay choose three traditions that belong to different families of religion. You should choose not only those traditions that best illustrate and support your definition, but also at least one tradition that challenges your definition. For example, if a fundamental part of your definition is belief in a personal Absolute, then you should consider how this definition could apply to early Buddhism, or Confucianism. Remember that one option you could pursue would be to argue that under your definition Tradition X does not qualify as a "religion" (that is to say, it is a "cultural tradition", a "political system", a "moral way of life", etc.) If you decide to present such an argument, however, you would need to consider the logical consequences of taking your position and the possible counter-arguments (such as the fact that Tradition X is identified as a "religion" in all the material you have studied).

Use this essay to take stock of your current thinking on the subject of "Religion", and to draw together the many ideas you have encountered this semester. Most of all, use it to point towards your future study and understanding of world religions.